The WHITBREAD
Rugby World '90

L

The WHITBREAD Rugby World '90

NIGEL STARMER-SMITH
AND IAN ROBERTSON

Lennard Publishing
1989

Lennard Publishing
a division of Lennard Books Ltd
Musterlin House
Jordan Hill Road
Oxford OX2 8DP

First published in 1989

This book is copyright under the Berne Convention
No reproduction without permission
All rights reserved

British Cataloguing-in-Publication Data
The Whitbread rugby world '90.
1. Rugby football
I. Starmer-Smith, Nigel, 1944– II. Robertson, Ian,
1945–
796.33'3

ISBN 1 85291 082 8

Design by Forest Publication Services
Printed and bound in Scotland by
The Eagle Press plc, Glasgow

The Editors wish to express their grateful thanks to the following for their help in the preparation of this book: Cathy Mancuso in Sydney and Alison Rusted in London for their organisation and administration of the copy; the excellent Sheraton Hotel in Brisbane for their kind co-operation; to Kewarra Resort for providing a peaceful haven for writing; Qantas and Cathay Pacific for superb services provided, and to Quicksilver Cruises for an unforgettable day with the Lions.

Thanks, too, to Adrian Stephenson of Lennard Publishing, as well as the tireless Bill Mitchell and Mrs Pat Symons of Rugby World and Post for all their efforts in helping to co-ordinate the operation from a distance, and to Colorsport, Ian Robertson and C. Henry for contributing the photographs, and Rod Jordan, his inimitable cartoons.

Personal gratitude of a high order is due to Leo Williams, President of Queensland Rugby Union for his unstinting generosity in Australia, together with so many players and officials, Lions and Australians, for their courteous contribution to our efforts.

Finally, and above all, especial thanks to Whitbread plc and in particular Paul Vaughan and Barrie Clarke, without whose continued support the publication of this book would not have been possible.

CONTENTS

FOREWORD
by CLIVE ROWLANDS O.B.E.
Manager British Isles Tour of Australia, 1989
President, Welsh Rugby Union.

"It's a long time since August 1988!" Those were the words with which Lions coach Ian McGeechan greeted me at the end of the emotion-sapping Third Test at Sydney Football Ground one year later. We had won the match and with it the first Test series victory for the British Isles for 15 years. There was a sense of relief, and a feeling of pride. The hard work and the careful preparation over many months had paid off.

Clive Rowlands as captain of Wales, meets Sir Alec Douglas Home.

It was in those early months of last season that the groundwork was laid. Carefully sifting through, with the important advice of the selection panel, the talent available from the Home Countries, plus the added advantage of being able to get some guidelines of what we could expect from the Wallabies as we saw them in action, first in defeat by England and then, by contrast, in comprehensive victory over Scotland and the Barbarians.

We learned much about their strengths and their limitations – and also about the playing resources available to us for the Lions tour.

So now it is that we can look back on victory that was not only most pleasing but a credit to the whole party. And I do mean the whole party – 32 players playing for each other and perhaps with not so many great stars as earlier successful Lions tours. There were similarities though to be seen with the preceding series win of 1974 in this particular element of player interdependence and mutual support.

The coaching work of Ian McGeechan and Roger Uttley was meticulous, laid down in their preparatory planning every evening before the following day's session. There was a purpose to everything they did and, because the players could see that there was a theme and object to what they did, there were never any grumbles from the tour party about having to turn out for practice almost every day, barring match days.

It was a hard tour; it's never easy to play a game as you might choose to do. Apart from your own abilities, there is also the opposition and the referees, and you have to adjust accordingly. Equally you play to your strengths and not just to entertain a crowd or the media when there is so much at stake. It was important to all of us, not just the touring team, that British Isles rugby should once again be seen to be successful.

It was also a very happy tour. Even when things were stressful, the squad pulled together. We had our days away from the rugby, and there was no shortage of fun, whether white-water rafting (frightening), relaxing in the Players' Court sessions, on the golf course, or marvelling at the Great Barrier Reef. Inevitably, there were personal disappointments but those were bravely borne. I respected the players, too, for the way they willingly undertook those other duties, visits to schools, clubs, and various functions which are incumbent upon a touring side – the sort of things which do not occur on the domestic international front or in a World Cup competition. It's a very different experience.

I would like to think that winning 'down under' will have given a boost to rugby in the Northern Hemisphere in general. I certainly believe that the next generation of young men who prepare themselves to take over the mantle as Lions tourists in Australia over the next 20 years or so will benefit from the fact that a British Isles team has been there and won a series. It is difficult to get out of a losing rut, but we have, and now we have finally won an international series in the Eighties as well.

I was once sceptical about the value of Lions tours in so far as I thought they

The British Lions' management face the press at the start of the tour; left to right, Roger Uttley, Clive Rowlands, Finlay Calder and Ian McGeechan.

would become of less importance with the advent of more and more tours overseas by individual nations. I now know that there remains a truly worthwhile validity to Lions touring. It has a value in itself for those taking part; it gives added interest to our own Home Internationals, and must surely reduce the chances of any acrimony occurring on the field when opponents are former team and room-mates on tour. It is also a proving ground for up-and-coming players, and by mixing the best players from the four countries the skill levels must improve as they learn from each other and the experience. At the same time the inter-relationship between players of different countries and the friendships made can only benefit the individual and rugby as a whole.

I hope the '89 Lions have helped to give touring sides more confidence abroad – winning away from home has been a problem for our national teams. Now we know once again that travelling to the Southern Hemisphere does not always mean defeat!

The high point of 1989 then was a very obvious one for me, and good news for British rugby. I hope you enjoy recalling in this book the way it happened, as well as looking forward with yet keener interest to another year of rugby.

Rugby football has always been a significant part of my life from my earliest village days in Cwmtwrch. The game is for fun, and yet it is intensely demanding physically and mentally; it is a man's game requiring courage and also great skill. It is a game which, well-nurtured, has a great future. But those future prospects will be enhanced or diminished by the lawmakers of the game. Somehow we have to simplify the complexities and the sooner we can get that done the better. Easier said than done I know!

Enjoy your season as player, official, administrator or spectator. Above all, have fun.

WHATEVER NEXT?

A Rugby Crisis
by ALAN JONES

Alan Jones, as a glossy Sydney fashion magazine recently put it, makes 'an unlikely sort of celebrity … but he is a middle-aged, middle-class hero.' Others have remarked that he appears to have been 'born at 40' (and he is now just 46) for he has become a renowned, controversial figure in Australia in a very short time. In rugby terms he has been Australia's most successful national coach of all time, masterminding the brilliant and unique Grand Slam triumph of the 1984 Wallabies in Britain before falling from public grace – as happens in Australia if you are associated with a losing team – during the first World Cup in 1987 when the national team failed to live up to expectations and finished only 4th. Hero or villain, even those stars in the Wallaby camp of yesteryear like Slack, Campese and Ella, who may not admit to liking the 'man', are unanimous in their appreciation of his coaching and motivating talents during Australia's finest hours.

Alan Jones in his Sydney home.

Aside from rugby, there is Jones the media-man, outspoken, self-publicising, a brilliant orator, witty, intensely interesting and hugely well informed. In thought, word and style he's more than a cut above your average Aussie. In fact he's so a-typical as to seem totally out of place. But he remains a star attraction as he tops the radio ratings with his 3-hour daily morning programme and is in constant demand as speaker, spokesman, interviewer and interviewee.

He's travelled an unusual road from a 'bush' farming family to a spell at teaching, a passing, yet on-going involvement as post-graduate and coach at Oxford University, to standing as an unsuccessful Liberal party candidate, to becoming Prime Minister Malcolm Fraser's speech-writer and policy adviser, to executive director of NSW Employers' Federation, to his present-day role as loved or despised media-man. Mind you, it's not only in Australia that a greater crime than being a failure is to be adjudged to be too successful.

In his magnificently-appointed home, an imaginatively-converted old factory, in which garish modern oils and watercolour paintings intermingle with rugby memorabilia on the walls, I asked him to ponder on the problems and the future of the sport of rugby union. One question was all that was required. I sat back and listened to this disturbing reply.

Nigel Starmer-Smith

The biggest weakness in international rugby remains still the prevailing concern that I had five years ago – and that is the gargantuan gulf between the administrators and the players. I spoke to a Test player the other day to convey a piece of information to him and he suggested we meet up for dinner and a chat, not knowing whether, after the Lions' Second Test victory, he would make the Wallaby side for the final Test of the series. I was able to inform him that the team had been selected six hours previously, and that he was still in the line-up. Had no one been in touch with him? Clearly not.

Then again, you talk to top players in leading international teams and ask what input they have into selection, are they consulted about itineraries on

Alan Jones in his days as Australian coach.

tours, and the demands on their time? Not a bit of it. There's the *cause célèbre*, which symbolises everything, of 'broken payment', where there's some presumption that if you are paid by the rugby authority for the period that you are playing for your country, that is alien to the spirit of the game.

As I have said repeatedly, what is most alien to me, however, is that officials never come away from home believing that they will have to forego income whilst on rugby travels. I remarked to one international official not long ago "Look, it's the age of burning the credit cards!" He said: "Yes, I agree, I retain only two these days: one is for my private use, the other just to keep everything nice and tidy, is to pay for my rugby expenses, which I then send in to the national Rugby Union and the charges are rebated." I suggested to him that that was most interesting and enquired of him what credit cards the players used to have their expenses rebated.

Eventually, players will find this kind of 'us and them' behaviour too much to swallow. I suggested five years ago that we were turning players into 'mobile banks'. What I said then applies equally now. There is something incongruous about the fact that 65,000 people can pack Twickenham, or 40,000 fill Sydney Football Stadium, or 50,000 at Cardiff Arms Park, whilst amongst the players on the pitch there are certainly some who endure pretty dire economic hardship.

No one expects to be paid for playing the game. But no one wants to be so far out of pocket that his financial circumstances disqualify him from playing the game. At the moment we say we are an amateur sport, but it is an absolutely professional environment within which we operate.

A programme is drawn up at the beginning of the year, or even years ahead. There is no consultation with senior players whatsoever. Yet, Saturday by Saturday, by Saturday, the top guys are playing a sequence of Test matches, provincial, regional or other representative fixtures. Over here it might be a succession which means playing against Auckland one week, Fiji the next, followed by Wellington, Canterbury, the Lions, Queensland, and so on.

And then, if we take the context of the British Lions tour, someone comes up with the great money-spinning idea of throwing in an extra full International, hence after three successive Test matches and the preceding provincial games, the tour ends with an Anzac game. The 'bank' just keeps moving on; that same mobile 'players' bank'.

Meanwhile one player doesn't pitch up for work on Monday because he's had his nose pushed in or his back put out, and an employer may not be best pleased. The cry goes up, "I'm not here to subsidise rugby".

It seems to me that the game has got to grow up. We go to the Hong Kong Sevens and we hear the most gratuitous remarks made by people who pass themselves off as international rugby authorities. You need only to listen to them sounding-off at the dinner table. They are unable to command the attention of the players, because what they are saying is irrelevant. You stand a 'revered' rugby official up to speak at the end of a banquet, (quiet please; respect the position, but for God's sake understand that he's talking nonsense!) – and he'll churn out what he regards as appropriate *bons mots* about the spirit of the game, and rugby being the winner.

Administrators in touch are few and far between. We had one here in NSW, Ross Turnbull, who had some access and lines of communication to the players because he was young and a respected former player. He's no longer in the game. I am sure you can think of others like him.

But with the present hierarchy I can only fear for where we are going in an international administrative sense.

The tight-knit exclusive members of the IRFB face a searching examination of their position in world rugby.

A few years ago we had a World Cup, and I said at the time that then was the time to put in place a World Secretariat for the game, to propagate rugby around the world. Isn't it nonsense that a nation participates in a World Cup by virtue alone of a gracious invitation extended by the supreme authorities of the International Rugby Board. What we should have had at the outset was a zonal competition, based on the lines of international soccer. Instead of which we have a situation in which Spain, or any other emerging rugby nation, is treated like a third-class citizen and excluded unless they express, as a precondition of taking part, a willingness to take on board all the requirements of the IRFB. There should be a zonal competition involving Spain, just as there should be one involving Romania, or Fiji or Malaysia. That's the only way to give internationality to the game.

We have another World Cup coming up, and it is based on the same elitist lines as existed for the last World Cup which failed to incorporate an holistic, open to all, total concept of a proper world competition. Consequently, the internationality of the game is compromised and sacrificed because the administrators cannot see far enough ahead.

The International Rugby Football Board, so called, comprises a handful of people with votes, whilst the remainder, Associate Members, are given what amounts to spectator status.

It's nonsense that Fiji and Argentina, for instance, can't vote! Give England five votes if need be, South Africa 10, New Zealand 20, whatever you like, but don't deny Spain, The Netherlands, USA, Western Samoa, Romania, Singapore, and everyone else the right to vote and have a say in contributing to the debate on the destiny of international rugby.

So I look back and cannot see any improvement in such things since I first made clear my views on the matter some years ago. Furthermore I think that the playing standards within the international game have deteriorated. You cannot expect the kind of commitment from players, or the enthusiasm that they have or ought to have, to continue to manifest itself if the player is isolated from any discussion about the future direction and destiny of rugby football.

There's a massive misconception about rugby in Australia. I don't know what it means to be 'rankly amateur'. But whatever perception is conjured up by those two words, we are it. I want to assure the international rugby community – and I've no stake in saying this – these players get nothing.

Now there might be – just might be – Michael Lynagh in Brisbane driving a car around and he might just have got the job because he's an outstanding goal-kicker and his company thought that to sell real estate or something they would put Michael Lynagh on their books. It could be that he might not have got the job were he not a prodigious goal-kicker. So one might conclude that there's a derivative value attaching to Michael Lynagh's job and his car. Beyond that, there's nothing to add.

Furthermore, there's no way, if we accepted broken time payment for international matches, that the game would become a professional game. But when a side forgathers for a Test match, and puts in days of preparation surely we are entitled to say to the players that as they are entertainers on a world stage, as they are going to perform before tens of thousands at the ground and even larger numbers on television, as they are going to bring in millions through gate receipts and sponsorship, so we are going to make sure that neither they nor their wives or families endure any economic hardship for the period that they are needed.

We have the choice. We either say that those players who would require and claim this financial assistance are cheats and dishonest, and are setting out to exploit the system, or we trust them and pay the legitimate out-of-pocket expenses incurred in playing for Australia, with a genuine interest in their well-being.

I can assure you that it is becoming increasingly difficult for players over here. I could go through the Australian squad and cite clear-cut instances of financial hardship exaggerated by rugby commitments, and if you add to that the alienation of players from the game because they perceive that it isn't moving in a sufficiently organised and professional way, then you will understand more clearly our problems.

The claims of rugby league are strong. The game has made gigantic strides in terms of its public presentation, with enormous press and television coverage. By contrast rugby union still does not have a television station truly

Two British defectors to rugby league: Alan Tait of Scotland (above) and Jonathan Davies of Wales (above right).

committed to the game, interested in presenting the product to a very enthusiastic and informed public. The Christian doctrine says, "Let your light so shine before men that they may see your good works". Obviously there are no Christians in the world of rugby, because they are not interested in letting anyone see the good works of their rugby players.

Eventually players say, as has happened here, enough's enough – Andrew Leeds swapped codes for a paltry $40, 000, that was enough to persuade him that the change was worthwhile. The kind of offers made to Michael Cook and Ricky Stuart were more substantial, but they didn't set out down a road that would take them to rugby league. They just got fed up.

Let me return to the case of the Rugby Football Union – and by that we are all meant to know that means England, (the pretension is breathtaking). The RFU seem to have taken up a position in which they feel they do not have to yield to pressure from the players, because such is the rugby patronage in Britain that they could put two dogs on the turf at Twickenham on a given date, call it a Test match, and 50,000 people would come to see it. They'd have their champagne and caviare in the car park, their fine wines in the Committee Room, and the hierarchy would look on from their privileged seats in the West Stand.

So, if there's a protest movement in England against the administration, the response would be along these lines – "If you don't want to play, old man, we'll get someone who does". That view prevails in Australia as well. It's only a couple of years back that a motion was moved by the Queensland Rugby Union to ban Codey and Slack from the game because, it seems, they caught a plane and went to South Africa and talked to a few people.

I would come back to a teaching analogy. You only ever realise that a teacher is hopeless as you are about to leave, and at that stage there's not much point in making a fuss about it. So the mediocrity and imperfection keeps perpetuating itself as the generations renew themselves. So it is for the rugby player, who only after a reasonable length of international rugby may finally come to realise that all is not good, and an alienation from the game is felt. It may have taken 20 Tests to find this out. The player decides to quit the game so as not to miss a career opportunity, and some marvellously keen young fellow from Bath or Bristol, Eastwood or Manly is only too happy to get his hands on an England or Wallaby jersey, at whatever cost to himself. He continues with vibrant enthusiasm until he notches up his 20 Tests, and then other thoughts and observations take over and he moves on the way of his predecessors, and so on. It's a self-generating process. It's one of the reasons why players are not continuing on the international scene to 30 and beyond.

Another cause of player dissatisfaction would seem to me also to stem from the failure of rugby authorities to rule their own destiny. I'm constantly tempted to ask the Australian Rugby Union if they have checked out the team for Saturday with Bob Hawke. In determining the international fixture list I get an impression that it is the Prime Minister who is the ultimate arbiter. We seem to bow and genuflect to the Government over matters of fundamental autonomy in relation to the administration of the game – namely whom we play, and where we go. I would have thought that there was no greater freedom available to us than freedom of association, and we are denying rugby footballers that very liberty. Is it simply that we are scared that it might have some bearing on the Olympics? Are we really saying that we must minister to the ambitions of the track and field athletes who will be competing at the next Olympic Games, but we are not entitled to minister to the ambition of every rugby player who wishes to play at Ellis Park or Newlands? You wait and see, at the next Olympics we'll be on the high beam competing against the Chinese gymnasts, whose regime has recently been responsible for mass murder in Tienanmen Square. There is so much hypocrisy. There would be a justification for taking your cue from your political leaders if their morality and intellectual integrity could be vouchsafed. Why cannot rugby be the architect of its own destiny?

If we had an expanded International Rugby Board, you would have an expanded power base from which to operate. If every country were party to the decision-making process in a world rugby community, it is far more likely that the political threats of an individual country could be ignored.

Sadly, it seems to me that it's axiomatic that the qualification for leadership in international rugby derives from a demonstrable perfection of a complete inability to lead – a complete inability to do the job you were elected to do. Once you're there you want the best seats in the synagogue, you want everyone to call you 'sir' and 'master', you make speeches after dinner, with no concern over the content or appeal, and you retain your self-perpetuating position. This is a tragedy, because rugby is full of intelligent, aware young men – but, because they've been ostracised from it and disenchanted as experienced internationals, hardly any have a wish to go back into the administration of the game. The people who do find their way into administration are largely those who never left their mark as players. The incentive required to keep people in the game is no longer there.

I'm pessimistic about rugby's future because we are betraying the ambition, the commitment and the talent of young people all around the world who are playing rugby.

It's not good enough to give someone an international jersey and say he's played in front of 50,000 people. He wants more than that – intellectual integrity. Honest, intelligent, rational answers to question which might range from "Why can't my dry cleaning bills be paid when I'm on international duty?" to "Why can't I have my salary paid for this week since I am forfeiting it by being involved in preparation for Saturday's Test match?" or "Why can't I play rugby in South Africa, when Evonne Goolagong, who is coloured, was allowed to play tennis there, or Ros Fairbank can appear in the Wimbledon semi-finals?" We have an obligation to the truth.

There's yet a further dimension to the overall problem, and that concerns refereeing. In the Supreme Court they will talk about truth in sentencing, and the sentence for murder, assault or possession of drugs must be a truthful reflection of the crime or the offence that has been committed against society. The same must apply to rugby refereeing and when adjudication takes place on the pitch, it must be a truthful representation of the relative merits and offences of each side. It's not happening. I find the standard of refereeing that the Lions suffered on their Australian tour personally embarrassing. The standard of international refereeing is not good enough. But where there are good men – the Clive Norlings of this world – they don't get near an international stadium these days.

Wherever you turn, there is quandary and dilemma. Rugby and its contemporary issues are not being addressed but are instead lost in the conviviality and camaraderie of the Unions' administrators.

THE LIONS
IN
AUSTRALIA

OPENING ENCOUNTERS AND THE FIRST TEST

by IAN ROBERTSON, BBC Rugby Correspondent

A week of splendid weather in the delightful surroundings of Perth and a 44–0 triumph over Western Australia seemed the ideal launching pad for the more serious hurdles ahead, but even in this relatively facile success the critics found some reason to be critical. Hardly any of this Lions team had played any competitive rugby since the end of April and it was scarcely surprising that they needed to dust off all the cobwebs and oil the various rusty areas before gliding into top form.Understandably there was a lot of scratching and scraping around as the team stumbled and scrambled to a half time lead of 8–0 against a very ordinary collection of honest, but not particularly talented, journeymen.

In the second half the motley assortment of guerillas who made up the Western Australian team gradually ran out of steam and ideas and the Lions cruised to a comfortable victory scoring nine tries and conceding none in the process. Unfortunately the style of this win set a pattern which the Lions pursued unwittingly right through to the start of the Test series. They played sluggishly and laconically for the first 40 minutes lacking imagination, cohesion and any sense of adventure or enterprise before raising the whole tempo dramatically in the second half to run out worthy winners.

Either at, or approaching, half-time in those next five matches they found themselves leading only 12–6 against Queensland 'B' and trailing in the others by margins of 14–7, 12–10, 9–7 and 6–3. Fortunately after these build-up matches, and at the half-way stage of the 12-match tour, they had scored a grand total of 25 tries whilst conceding only seven. However, the unpalatable fact remained that they had failed to play well in the first half in a single match and had only shown any semblance of true international form in the second half.

There is no simple explanation to what was a complex problem but various contributory factors help to explain the dilemma which confronted two very experienced and, each in their own way, outstanding coaches, Ian McGeechan and Roger Uttley. Apart from England, who had thrashed Romania in an exercise romp in the middle of May, the fact remained that the squad of players had had no competitive play for around six weeks before the opening match in Perth and there was an inevitable lack of match fitness. It should be remembered that previous Lions tours in recent times have started in mid-

May and have not had to overcome this particular playing hiatus.

There also followed the usual Lions problem at the outset of a tour of trying to weld the cosmopolitan talents of four different and separate nations into one united team. This involved reaching a negotiated compromise on whether to ruck or maul as a general rule, because the different nations at home hold conflicting views on this crucial issue.

The particular problem facing the coaches was the fact that the First Test came after just six matches and then with the three Tests in successive weeks there was very little margin for error. In such a tight schedule a crop of injuries to key players immediately exacerbated what was already a hard tour.

With three weeks from the first match to the First Test every game and every individual performance counted. The loss of Paul Dean in Perth through injury left a huge responsibility on the capable shoulders of the young but very talented fly-half Craig Chalmers. The forwards, hesitant initially, were totally dominant in the end against Western Australia. Their efforts were rewarded with some glorious running from Brendan Mullin (3 tries), Rory Underwood (2) and Scott Hastings (1). The service from Robert Jones at scrum-half provided the ideal catalyst to unleash the backs in the second half.

In the second match on a sodden pitch on a wet night in Melbourne, with a slippery ball, the only highlight was the performance of the pack, full of

Photocall for the Lions against the impressive backdrop of the Syndey Harbour Bridge.

naked aggression and selfless physical commitment. They wore down Australia 'B' and were able to grind out a victory which was much more comfortable than the 23–18 margin might suggest. Armstrong hoisted a series of towering, tormenting kicks which kept the Lions going forward and made life very unpleasant for the home team. In atrocious conditions the Lions adapted well and played sensible effective percentage rugby.

The first watershed came in Brisbane with the match against Queensland who had enjoyed a great season, including two wins over New South Wales in which they scored over 30 points each time. With a team not that far removed from the one intended for the First Test, the Lions took most of the first half to find their rhythm and build up sufficient momentum to subdue the Queensland forwards and take tactical control of the match. This they achieved with another abrasive, but disciplined, performance from the pack. Sole, Moore and Young broke the Queensland front row and had them hanging on for dear life late on. Ackford, Norster and Richards won much more quality line-out possession and Teague, in particular, was immense in the loose. The defensive organisation of the Lions, which went to pieces in the First Test, was exemplary on this occasion and restricted Queensland to five penalties from Michael Lynagh. Robert Jones scored the only try of the game and the only other real threat of tries came from the Lions. Chalmers dropped two goals and Gavin Hastings kicked three penalties but there was an element of disappointment that, with the pack storming forward, the back division achieved relatively little. The very few moves which were attempted were done at half pace running laterally across the pitch and posing no real danger. On the credit side the crunching forward power of the Lions had proved far too much for Queensland and augered well for the Test series.

The match in Cairns was another amorphous mess in the first half but a brilliant break by Rob Andrew just before half-time, well supported by Jerry Guscott led to a spectacular try by Chris Oti to transform the game. The Lions' pack yet again outplayed and outgunned the opposition and three more tries followed to leave Queensland 'B' well beaten.

The Lions then found surprising and unexpected resistance against New South Wales and despite more heroics from their forwards, they saw a comfortable lead of 20 points to 12 disappear in a magnificent New South Wales recovery which saw the home side snatch a 21–20 lead in injury time. The situation was retrieved only when Craig Chalmers dropped his third goal of the match in the third minute of injury time. Despite the high drama of the thrilling finish, the Lions were clearly the better team and having beaten Queensland and New South Wales on successive Saturdays there seemed plenty of justification to hope that they could inflict similar damage

David Campese on the attack.

on their combined strength in the First Test.

The Dubbo match in mid-week meant little. A facile win 39–19 was again largely due to the efforts of the Lions forwards although the backs had their moments in the second half with Mike Hall, Rory Underwood and Rob Andrew all having good games. With their unbeaten record intact, the Lions flew back to Sydney full of confidence as they prepared for the most important examination of their skill – the First Test. They could have done with another week but they had the consolation of knowing that Australia would be playing their first international together for seven months and the only worry for the Lions was the extent of their injuries.

THE FIRST TEST

When the Lions came to name their team they confirmed that five of their squad were not considered because of injury. Donal Lenihan had played well at the start of the trip but even if he had been fit he would probably not have been chosen ahead of Paul Ackford. On the other hand Mike Teague was certain to have been chosen at blind-side flanker, Chris Oti could have expected selection on the wing and the Lions management had never tried to conceal the fact that Scott Hastings and John Devereux were the first choice pairing in the centre.

Despite all the efforts of the team 'physio', Kevin Murphy, who worked wonders in cutting the time players were out through injury to the very bare minimum, the Lions were forced to go into the First Test without any of these five players, at least four of whom would have been their first-choice selections. On a gloriously sunny afternoon a capacity crowd of 40,000 were packed into the relatively new all-seater Sydney Football Stadium to watch the battle of giants.

For the Lions it was to be a day of deep disappointment and depression which was made much harder to accept because the whole team knew that they had failed to do themselves justice or anything like it. The pack had played so well and had been so dominant and outstanding throughout the whole tour that the players seemed to have got into a frame of mind where they felt they could not lose the Test.

They had proved vastly superior to all four of the combined sides they had met and they were also a cut above both Queensland and New South Wales, and it seemed perfectly reasonable to expect them to be too powerful for the Wallaby pack which was after all only an uneasy alliance of the best of the two state sides.

The mistake the Lions made was to assume their dreams would be fulfilled even if they failed to reproduce the fierce abrasive physical forward play which had pulverised the opposition right through the month of June. Instead of increasing the tempo the Lions relaxed the pace and paid the penalty. It is very difficult to begin a match in first gear and then suddenly explode into top gear.

The Lions were outplayed in the line-out where Australia won more quality possession. The Wallabies were thought to be slightly fragile in the set scrums, but Lions domination in this key area failed to materialise and in the open the Wallabies were quicker to the breakdown over and over again which gave those brilliant half-backs, Nick Farr-Jones and Michael Lynagh, the perfect platform to take total control of the match. With Miller, Tuynman and Gourley well on top at the rucks and mauls, Lynagh was able to dictate the whole course of the match and this he did to great effect. His line and tactical kicking were almost faultless and he also had the insight and imagination to unleash the three quarter line at precisely the right time. His variation of tactics was an object lesson for any budding fly-half and he did a great deal to break down the Lions' resistance.

The major problem for the Lions, after an encouraging opening ten minutes, was that so many of their players had an off-day. In the final analysis at least ten and possibly twelve of the team played well below their best and this collective catastrophe virtually guaranteed defeat.

They spent most of the match on the retreat, playing the game off the back foot and the overwhelming, driving, aggressive forward play which had been a characteristic feature of every match up to the Test never surfaced or even threatened to surface.

Far left New Zealand referee Keith Lawrence lays down the law to Brian Moore in the presence of Finlay Calder.
Left David Sole and Paul Ackford found the going harder than expected in the First Test.
Below Michael Lynagh challenges Gavin Hastings to prevent the threat of a Lions counter-attack.

With the pack crumbling in front of them, the backs were unable to influence the match and they ended up looking just as tentative, hestitant and unsure of themselves as the forwards. In all fairness it must be emphasised that Australia played exceptionally well and thoroughly deserved their victory, but it was frustrating for the Lions who knew they had been well below par.

The Australian loose-forwards and half-backs had laid the foundations of a splendid victory and they took great delight from the fact that the British Lions in all their classic Test battles against New Zealand and South Africa this century had only twice previously lost by a bigger score than the 30–12 drubbing inflicted on them in Sydney.

The try count of four tries to none further underlined the extent of the damage suffered by the Lions whose 12 points came from four kicks – two by Gavin Hastings and two by Craig Chalmers. For Australia, Lynagh kicked one penalty and one drop goal and converted all four tries scored by Walker, Gourley, Maguire and Martin. It was a comprehensive win for the Wallabies but even they were surprised by the timidity of the Lions and they acknowledged afterwards that they had caught the tourists on a real off-day and could not count on such a lack lustre performance again.

REFLECTIONS OF THE TWO CAPTAINS

Nick Farr-Jones I said to the players in the build-up to this Test that, if we did all the basic things well and were all committed to working flat out together for victory, we could beat this Lions team even though they had put in some very good performances earlier in the tour, especially against Queensland and New South Wales. I emphasised that we had to be faster round the pitch in the open and we had to be well-organised both in attack and defence. I think we used the shortened line-out to our advantage on many occasions and our pack scrummaged really well. Most critics felt the Lions would out-scrummage us in this Test just as they had in the Queensland game but we worked very hard to make sure this did not happen and it was one of the main reasons we won. A solid scrum and far more possession at the rucks and mauls gave us exactly the platform we needed and I don't think there is any doubt our forwards outplayed the Lions. In the dressing-room before the match I told the forwards that if they won quality possession in the scrums and line-out then we would be able to dominate in the loose, and play the game in the Lions' half of the field and the points would come sooner or later. With the help of some tremendous loose-forward play and some great kicking by Michael Lynagh and Greg Martin, that is exactly what happened and by varying our tactics sensibly we always had the edge over the Lions. Another difference between the teams was that we were able to capitalise on every opportunity we created which helped us to score four tries. Winning Test matches is so often simply about taking every opportunity. I've been fortunate to have played in several great Australian victories at international level during the last six years, starting with the 1984 Grand Slam tour of Britain and including wins over the All Blacks, but this triumph would have to be right up there among the great Wallaby performances in recent years.

Finlay Calder My own immediate impressions looking back on this First Test are a mixture of bitter disappointment at the result and the way we played and sheer frustration that, after so many good efforts on the tour, we should produce easily our worst performance so far, especially the first 40 minutes, in the most important game. In simple terms we were not quite as totally committed and determined as we should have been and the Australians were. We didn't take our early chances and the Wallabies did later on, we missed kicks at goal and the Wallabies didn't, and the explosive fiery thundering forward power which had broken all opposition in the first six games was missing when we needed it most. I think we were perhaps guilty of believing we couldn't lose instead of making certain that we did everything flat out to guarantee victory. We made far too many mistakes and we failed to realise our full potential. If I'm going to be honest I have to admit that we did not deserve to win. We were not hungry enough on the day to make sure we would win and, as often happens, the Wallabies as underdogs, written off by most people, rose magnificently to the challenge, fired by the burning desire to prove everyone wrong. This is not an excuse on our part, but a criticism. At the same time, we must give full credit to the Australians for hitting peak form in their first international of 1989. The sad truth is that we beat ourselves because too many of the team as individuals played poorly, and collectively we failed to fire on all cylinders. As I sat in the changing-room afterwards I can say without any doubt that I had never before been so disappointed, depressed and dejected after a rugby match.

Everything went wrong for us and went right for them. The kicking and general play of Farr-Jones, Lynagh and Martin was soul-destroying for us even though it is probably fair to say their pack won the Test for them. Next week I guarantee we will be far, far more committed and a week is long enough to put matters right. Sometimes if you have a month or a year before setting out on the retrieving mission you might forget how painful the defeat was but we won't be thinking of anything else for the next seven days and I can promise you it will be completely different next Saturday in Brisbane. These Lions will never play so badly again!

A WEEK IN THE LIFE OF GAVIN HASTINGS

Saturday 1st July. Sydney.
Australia 30 British Isles 12

Sunday 2nd July. Sydney.
The morning after the day before! An acceptance that we had let ourselves down in the First Test. It seemed we had 'frozen' on the day and although I felt the preparation had been good, little went right on the day. It can happen. I believe that it wasn't so much Australia winning the match, well though they had played, as us losing it. It had all come as a nasty surprise which only served to heighten our resolve. The rehabilitation began with the Saturday night Court Session under Judge Donal Lenihan and Chief Prosecutor Brian Moore. There hasn't been a 'Not Guilty' verdict yet!

Sunday was a day off to relax and unwind. I went back with some of the lads to the Sydney Football Stadium to indulge in the marvellous facilities, some swimming, a bit of weight-training, squash, sauna and jacuzzi. It helped to erase the nightmare events of the previous day. Then it was lunch with my brother, Scott, before another piling of belongings into the suitcase and off to the airport for the afternoon flight to Canberra.

Monday 3rd July. Canberra.
An important training session, quite intensive, going through areas of the game in which we had failed on Saturday – ball-winning and ball-retention for the forwards; positional play and tactical play for the backs. Then the Tuesday side to play ACT went through their game plan and teamwork.

Lunch was laid on for us at Daramalan rugby club, with typical local hospitality, and then a group of us visited the Australian Institute of Sport, which appropriately is at Bruce. It's an impressive set-up, combining a wide range of excellent facilities together with the appropriate staffing to give the coaching instruction required for Australia's best athletes. Since 1980, when it was established, the Institute has hosted all Australia's top sportsmen and women, with nominated athletes receiving scholarships which provide them with board, educational allowance, training and competition, clothing and equipment, coaching, domestic and international travel, as well as the support services provided by sports science and medicine. Rugby is one of the most recent sports to have become fully established at the Institute, and training programmes for Australia U–21 are currently being supervised there. Swimming, gymnastics, tennis, soccer and hockey, as well as other indoor sports are superbly catered for. An impressive set-up. Interesting to visit.

It was back on the social circuit in the evening, as guests of the British High Commission, which turned out to be more of a pleasure than a duty.

Tuesday 4th July. Canberra.

The lasting memory of today (especially for Dean Richards whose nose it got up in particular) was of a 'song' – if you can call it that: "We are the boys from the ACT, kookaburras, kookaburras, 1, 2, 3" which was played *ad nauseam* at every stoppage or scoring break throughout the match in the afternoon, blasted over the public address. We could have done without that.

Before the match, though, there was a 'dirt-trackers' morning training session as usual, for those not in the team or on the bench. Then out to the Sieffert Oval, at Queanbeyan – a rugby league ground, for the match, and an uncomfortable experience – at least for half the match!

With the Lions looking for a morale-booster it wasn't looking too clever for quite a while – 18–4 down after 22 minutes, 21–11 at half-time. But it was then that the lads showed real character to dig themselves out of trouble and pile on 30 points in the second half to win. The Press didn't give us much credit for the win but I felt it gave us quite a boost in our build-up to the Test.

This evening at the after-match function there was a dinner rather than the usual drinks and snacks reception, which are the norm in Australia and New Zealand. It was held in the Civic Centre in Queanbeyan with all the local dignitaries, players, officials and wives. That's probably why we had to go up on stage for a sparkling rendition of the tour song, 'Wild Mountain Thyme'. Well I thought it was sensational, anyway – at least on a par with the rugby choir that followed. The evening/early morning concluded in the swish new Raiders (rugby league) night-club. That was OK.

Wednesday 5th July. Brisbane.

Basically a travel day with a dreaded early start. But I'm not complaining. The hotels have been good – for once the Press have not been getting the better deal they usually claim! So conditions have been comfortable, travel arrangements fine and I've not felt over-burdened with off-field commitments and functions. They're all part and parcel of touring – albeit relaxing days are few and far between. A couple of days off at Surfers Paradise next week will be welcome. So an early flight today, change of planes in Sydney, a short delay, and on to Brisbane. Into the hotel, a quick bite and off to training 50 minutes later. No respite. From the local club ground where we trained it was back to the same club for an early evening barbecue with a large gathering of rugby folk, and especially school-kids. It was well organised with the youngsters grouped together by their playing positions. At table I was surrounded by fullbacks, but enjoyed their enthusiasm and interest in the game.

I can sense already the positive attitude building up in the Lions camp, as we head towards Saturday. With just one match in focus now it is important to get the rest hours in, so an early night is no bad thing.

Thursday July 6th. Brisbane.

An important training session at Brisbane Boys College, quite long and intensive, and the final major work-out prior to the Test. A superb setting in the sub-tropical surroundings, and marvellous facilities, plus plenty of local enthusiasm. I think the whole school must have turned out to watch us, and you've never seen a bigger crowd follow a pack's session on a scrummage machine! We knew the Test side and the five changes, although the selection had not been officially announced at that stage. The mood was good, there was no sense of panic, and our dented pride had prompted us to respond as a team and rebuild the required self-confidence. As usual I ended the session with some practice place-kicks.

With Nigel Starmer-Smith at Brisbane Boys College.

It was a glorious afternoon, and a chance to relax in the open air. I had a late lunch and went up to the roof-top pool, relaxed, read a book and had a chat with some of the other lads. It was good to have an evening 'off' as well. There was a dinner on but Saturday's team were excused attending. So instead, we had a quiet meal together and watched a video of the First Test. Not great to review but necessary. We talked about it and set our sights on what we needed to do to make amends in the next Test. Equally important was the relaxation itself; I think it's important to reduce your commitments and not rush around prior to a big match. Preparation is a gradual thing. We have thought long and hard about how we have to improve on the last week. There was a great resolve and determination.

Friday 7th July. Brisbane.

A light run-around and the need for keen concentration and everything to go smoothly. It worked out very well. We didn't train for too long, about 25 minutes at the same venue. I practised some more kicking at the end of the session because obviously I was anxious to improve on last Saturday's efforts. It's a funny thing, though, about place-kicking. The day before a 'game' you can kick 20 out of 20, when there's no-one watching you, but come the day with a vast crowd and the tension of the occasion, you can miss the lot – or vice versa. No rhyme nor reason. Practice, though, can only help and so I have made a point of doing plenty of extra work at each training session.

I am happy with the way things have been going, and am confident I have put things on an even keel. I don't mind the responsibility that the kicker has to take on.

For the week Mike Griffiths has been my room-mate, and it has worked out well. I approve of the mixing up of players though, of course, in the Test week the team and replacements room together in pairs. It's all an important part of the Lions' concept which only Bob Norster and Donal Lenihan have experienced before. The integration of players and nationalities can only have long term, as well as short term, benefits for the game, as well as enhancing the whole touring experience. We all realise that it's something different and special and not available to anyone else – a short period in your life that you will always cherish. Unique indeed, to the four home nations and a one-off event for almost all the players.

It was a good break from the rugby to pay a visit later in the day to the Brisbane offices of the company I work for in London, Richard Ellis, surveyors and estate agents, who have a big presence out here. It was an enjoyable lunch in some different company, taking my mind off the Test match, and that's important now and again.

The evening also provided some distraction. I enjoy the cinema and we went *en bloc* to a movie called *Dead Con* – a thriller, which wasn't bad. And so to bed early, and a good night's sleep.

Saturday 8th July. Brisbane.

What a great day and what a relief!

Up at 9 am, breakfast, the papers to read and, as I like to do, a quiet stroll on the morning of the match, with Craig Chalmers for company.

Back for a team meeting at 11.30 am, and good to see brother Scott alongside. A special day ahead I hoped, both for us and for my parents who had arrived to see the match. Saturday mornings always seem to drag a bit and to my mind, in the end, kick-off can't come soon enough.

Some apprehension, but a calm, confident feeling in the camp, a determined air, based on belief in our ability, a short drive to the ground, arriving about an hour and ten minutes before kick-off. The curtain-raiser was on, there was a good crowd and no rush; time to soak in the atmosphere.

All the time, thoughts on what we have to do, and mentally recapping on what we need to concentrate on. As Ian McGeechan had stressed, the requirement was to keep the ball in front of the forwards, making sure the backs were crossing the gain line whenever the ball was presented to us – allowing the back row to break off and cut loose in a forward direction.

And that we managed to do; it was those areas which to me represented the great differences between the two Tests. This time we had Australia on the back foot most of the time and that was crucial to us in winning the game. And then there was the restoration of confidence; you've only to look at the quality of the players in the side to know that, playing to form, we had to have a very good chance of winning. Test matches are so often won on small things and we knew we hadn't done ourselves justice in the First Test. We made a lot of mistakes. Not so the second time round and there was real satisfaction in the turnover of the results.

Post-match, a quick vocal effort in the dressing room, a quiet reception in the Murrayfield Room (a hospitality room at Ballymore first used to entertain a Scotland touring team!); short, quiet speeches reflecting, I think, the effort that had gone into the game. It had, after all, been a very physical, hard game. And the laurels belonged to us.

A few drinks back at the Mayfair Crest, our team hotel, before dinner, and then, for some, celebrations out on the town; for others like myself, an early night brought on by sheer fatigue.

Postscript

Looking back I have no doubts that we deserved to win. Although time was running out, there was never any sense of panic, we kept plugging away, kept cool, and earned the reward in those last five minutes. After all, we played as well at the tail end as at any other time in the match. This time they gave way, we didn't.

Many have said it was a brutal game. One or two early incidents apart – and one especially involving David Young – it was little different in that respect from other Tests I've played in. It was hard; but rugby is tough going 'down under' and on this tour it was so from the very start. People seem to forget one or two of the things that happened to us earlier in the tour. We weren't going to be subdued. We learnt the lessons.

Life on tour.
Above left My battle with the rapids.
Left An impromptu swim for some Lions after capsizing.
Above Midweek golf in Cairns.
Below left Pre-match build-up in Sydney.
Below My room-mate Mike 'Cecil B. de Mille' Griffiths.

THE SECOND TEST
by IAN ROBERTSON

The midweek match between the First and Second Tests promised to be a serious examination of the resolve and character of the Lions following the disaster at the Sydney Football Stadium. The record of the Australian Capital Territory team against touring sides looked most imposing – it included victories over Wales, Italy, Argentina, Fiji and Japan, a draw with France, and a narrow defeat against the All Blacks.

When ACT led the Lions 21–11 after 40 minutes , a second embarrassing defeat in a week seemed a decided possibility but, once again, a second-half transformation enabled the Lions to stage a dramatic recovery and win very comfortably in the end.

The Lions coach, Ian McGeechan, admitted afterwards that the first half was the Lions' worst 40 minutes of the whole tour up to that point but he was satisfied at full time with a winning margin of 41–25.

With the Lions pack in total charge throughout the second half it was disappointing for the crowd in Canberra that the Lions scarcely used their backs even when the game was won for sure. Indeed, the last three scores, with ACT floundering on the ropes, compeletely helpless having played themselves to a standstill, were three penalty goals by Peter Dods.

This was a sad indictment on the Lions' approach and ignored the fact that the Lions' backs individually and collectively were vastly superior to their relatively humble opponents. I am convinced that if the Lions had run the ball in the last half-hour they would probably have scored an extra 20 or 30 points; but in their defence the management can justifiably point out that tactically they played in Canberra exactly how they intended to play in Brisbane in the Second Test and it could be regarded as good practice.

The Test team was announced on the Friday and it showed five changes from the previous Saturday. In the pack Wade Dooley and Mike Teague took over from Bob Norster and Derek White. In the backs the whole mid-field trio was changed, with Craig Chalmers, Mike Hall and Brendan Mullin making way for Rob Andrew, Scott Hastings and Jerry Guscott. Apart from changing five players, much more significant was the fact that the whole attitude and approach by the Lions had also changed. The taunts in the local press about the toothless Lions being easily tamed in Sydney had struck a raw nerve and no one watching the team train on the final days leading up to the Second Test was in any doubt that the Wallabies were in for a rude shock if

The full weight of the law, in the shape of PC Wade Dooley, about to descend on Nick Farr-Jones.

Above Celebration as Jerry Guscott scores to clinch the Lions victory.
Above right It takes three Australians to halt Dean Richards.
Above far right Rory Underwood races past Ian Williams.

they expected the Lions to roll over and have their tummies tickled again.

And so it proved. The docile, hesitant, complacent, couchant Lions of Sydney were transformed into the rampaging, roaring, rampant Lions of Brisbane – the Kings of the Jungle. Unfortunately, there were a few moments when the Ballymore pitch in Brisbane did indeed resemble a jungle, but these should be put in perspective. In the first half it was occasionally an ill-tempered match with players resorting to violence, as both teams were psyched up to such an extent that a minor incident was likely to spark off a major outburst.

Punches were swopped at early line-outs and at one of the first scrums there was an amazing scene as Robert Jones nudged against Farr-Jones' left boot as he was about to put the ball into the scrum and, when Farr-Jones elbowed him aggressively out of the way, Robert Jones was quick to retaliate. In a trice the two scrum-halves were furiously wrestling and fighting on the ground with the helpless, hapless and, in terms of discipline, weak referee René Hourquet trying to prise them apart. In a split second while this was going on the scrum had broken up and the forwards were also slugging it out.

With players living on short fuses for the rest of the game, there were inevitably one or two other flare-ups which, equally inevitably, provoked retaliation and further ugly scenes. However, the whole match was certainly not spoiled by these examples of indiscipline even though, with the unease between the two teams bubbling away under the surface right through the match, the liklihood of unpleasant incidents was always there and that is not the right atmosphere in which to play international rugby.

Arguably the most unpleasant act of dangerous play came when the Lions prop David Young stood on Steve Cutler's head at a ruck which led to a furious reaction from Wallaby hooker, Tom Lawton, who let fly at the Lions players, punching in every direction. The referee had missed the original offence and had to hear about it second-hand from the New Zealand touch judge, and he appeared to have difficulty in understanding the full implication of what had happened.

The media focussed on this and other incidents during the next few days. Tom Lawton was quoted at length in Australian papers branding the Lions as hooligans, before condemning his own involvement in the fracas.

In his weekly Australian newspaper column the highly respected former Wallaby fly-half, Mark Ella, also jumped on the media bandwaggon in lambasting David Young in particular and the British Lions in general. His outspoken comments further fuelled the controversy which dragged on during the following week and which did not do the image of rugby any good.

The relevant facts were quite straightforward. The Australian press and players conveniently ignored the handful of flare-ups in some of the earlier tour matches in which Australian players had been seen in a poor light. The awful raking Julian Gardner inflicted on Mike Hall was never mentioned, nor

Below Dooley dominates the line-out. **Below left** Greg Martin finds himself isolated by the Lions forwards.

the treatment handed, or rather booted out, to Mike Teague and Gavin Hastings, nor a few other unpleasant and untoward incidents.

Secondly, apart from the few outbreaks of trouble already touched upon and, of course, in no way condoned, the Second Test, especially the second half, was not a dirty game. It must be emphasised that it was very hard and very physical but also perfectly fair. The over-reaction by the media in the aftermath has be to put into context.

The Lions management made it clear that they regretted the trouble when the manager, Clive Rowlands, reprimanded David Young for his part in the main unsavoury incident. In all this hurly burly the match developed into a fierce battle of wills between the two sets of forwards and there was very little constructive back play from either side. But let me repeat that, apart from the half-a-dozen occasions when players were undoubtedly ill-disciplined, it was the sort of typical bruising, physical forward contest we come to expect at Test match level all over the world and there was no justification for the Australian press to protest so vehemently about it being a disgracefully rough match.

The furious, fierce, aggressive, abrasive forward play of the Lions was perfectly legal and ruthlessly, clinically effective. They showed a shuddering commitment to driving the Wallabies backwards at every ruck and maul, shoulders low and legs pumping just like the great All Black forwards of recent years. Gradually and relentlessly, they wore down the Australian pack and outplayed them to such an extent that they won three times as much ball in the open which proved critical in the final analysis. Calder, Richards and Teague were superb in the loose and they comprehensively outplayed their opponents. Robert Jones and Rob Andrew controlled the Second Test with all the composure and tactical skill that Farr-Jones and Lynagh had displayed the previous week. The kicking of both Jones and Andrew was outstanding and yet when the crunch came at the very end of the match they knew when to release the three quarters.

Lynagh had kicked two penalties and converted an early try by Greg Martin after just quarter of an hour to leave Australia leading 12–6 mid-way through the second half. In the final 15 minutes the Lions hit back to add to the first half penalty by Gavin Hastings and the drop goal by Rob Andrew. Andrew landed a penalty and then, in the final few thrilling and dramatic minutes, the whole Test series was turned upside down as first Gavin Hastings and then Jerry Guscott scored tries to give the Lions a well-deserved hard-fought victory. Both these tries came from running the ball in the backs in the opposition '22' and this proved that the Lions could capitalise on half an opportunity and make something out of very little when the outcome of the tour depended on it.

In this Test the Lions were the more committed side even if they began in rather frenetic fashion, hunting and hassling the Wallabies to knock them out of their stride; by the end they had produced a regal forward performance of consummate authority to square the series, restore British pride and set up the perfect climax back in Sydney for the final Test.

The Lions had won a game of high emotion and passion and they had put right out of their minds all the gloom and doom of the previous week. They had proved in emphatic style that the reports from Syndey after the First Test of the death of British rugby had been greatly exaggerated. They had steamrollered the Wallabies right out of the match with a pulverising performance of forward power, ably supported by the half-backs, Jones and Andrew. They had not only redressed the balance; they had installed themselves as firm favourites for the final Test.

AFTER MATCH REFLECTIONS

Gavin Hastings When the final whistle went I had a feeling of great relief rather than one of euphoric celebration. It was a desperately hard-fought match and for the Lions there was tremendous satisfaction in turning the tables on the Wallabies, even though it took us until the last few minutes to get the crucial scores. I believe we deserved to win and I can honestly say that despite trailing 12–9 approaching full-time I never sensed we were running out of time and the team had no feeling of panic. Our concentration and determination near the end of the match were as high as at any other time. As for it being a brutal game; all I can say is it was hard, very hard and physical but I certainly didn't get the impression it was dirty. Apart from a couple of incidents it was no different, no better, and no worse than most of the internationals in which I've played.

Finlay Calder I think it was a fantastic effort for the Lions to come back from the disappointment of last week's defeat to win this Test. The pack played magnificently and I think the turning point came when the Wallaby prop, Dan Crowley, caught a kick-off and the Lions pack frog-marched him and the rest of the Australian pack backwards for 25 yards in double quick time. In that one act, we asserted our forward supremacy and we never looked back. It was a tactical triumph for the Lions at the end of a very hard, very competitive, keenly fought game.

Dean Richards It definitely was not the roughest or toughest game I've played in this season. The French match at Twickenham was far more physically demanding and I've played in several other internationals which have been tougher. It was a typically hard forward contest full of commitment.

Ian McGeechan It was a great fillip for British rugby to play so well in this Test after being so disappointing in the First Test. I thought the forwards were terrific and I completely reject the Australian media's accusation that we needed to resort to rough-house tactics to square the series. There were a few moments in the first half when players overstepped the mark, but otherwise it was just another furiously contested international. In all international rugby nowadays players ruck and maul with no quarter asked or given and, just as the great All Black teams never take a step backwards when the going gets tough, neither did the Lions or the Wallabies in this Test.

Roger Uttley   The forwards learnt the lessons of the First Test and the Australians found us a completely different proposition this time. We outplayed them in every aspect of forward-play and the psychological advantage must be with us going into the deciding game next week. Tonight I am very relieved and also very confident that we will win the series in Sydney.

Tom Lawton I was incensed at some of the things the Lions did in this match. At times they behaved like hooligans and the best word to describe it is thuggery. If that is the price to be paid for winning then I want no part of it. What a tragedy it would be if someone ended up with their brains scrambled after taking a deliberate kick in the head. When I saw David Young stamp on Steve Cutler I wasn't going to let the incident go by, but acting as I did (charging into the ruck with fists flying) was the most embarrassing moment of my rugby career. These are not the principles by which I play rugby. The hardest game an Australian rugby player can play is against the All Blacks. They are twice as hard as the Lions but you know nothing is going to happen off the ball against the Kiwis.

Nick Farr-Jones   I think the Third Test could develop into open warfare. As far as I'm concerned the Lions have now set the rules and set the standards and if the officials are not going to control the match then we're going to have to do something ourselves. We won't sit back and cop it again.

Mark Ella Head-kicking has to be one of the lowest acts ever committed on a rugby field and for the game's good it has to be eliminated immediately. Rugby does not need this type of animal behaviour.

Dominic Maguire I now know all about the ups and downs of international rugby. After my Test début last week I was a hero. Today I missed a tackle on Gavin Hastings when he scored the winning try and now I am a villain.

René Hourquet If I consider someone should be sent off, they will be sent off. But this match was not a violent match. It was a very physical game but it was certainly not violent. If you could erase the two painful moments in the first half it was a match without any problems at all.

'CAMPO'

A Rugby Way of Life
by DAVID CAMPESE

Mark Ella has described David Campese as "One day 'wonderman', next day 'blunderman'". At age 26, by the end of the Lions '89 tour of Australia, he had won 45 caps for the Wallabies, a total number of appearances second only to Simon Poidevin (47 caps) in Australian rugby history, had scored 32 international tries (a world record), and yet in the minds of his fellow countrymen he has remained both hero and villain.

As wing-threequarter or fullback, he has certainly touched the extreme heights and plumbed the very depths on the international rugby field. What greater contrast could there be within so short a span of time than 'Campese, the incomparable artist', in action against Scotland and the Barbarians whilst on the Wallaby tour of the UK in November 1988, and just three Test matches later, 'Campo the Culprit', as the player adjudged to have cost Australia the Test series against the Lions with his critical error in the decisive Third Test in Sydney in July 1989?

A naturally-gifted athlete, David Campese has enjoyed more of a life in rugby

David Campese with fellow Wallabies Mark Ella (left) and Andy Slack celebrating their Grand Slam in 1984.

union than any other player for, aside from the normal round of commitments with club, state and country, and six major overseas tours in four years, he has chosen to play 'off-season' each year in Italy, not only prompting allegations of professionalism but also ensuring that his working career has been a secondary priority in his life.

In every sense the individualist, his desire to be a free agent on and off the field has put him sometimes on a collision course with coaches and administrators. His views on the game he lives and loves emphasise the unique appeal and character of one of the world's great players.
Nigel Starmer-Smith.

Always a difficult man to stop.

I was like any other kid. A small-town guy in a population of 24,000 in Queanbeyan, near Canberra on the borders of Australian Capital Territory. In fact it's more rugby league territory – home of the Canberra Raiders, who play in the top competition. So at school it was mainly league, cricket, golf, you name it, I had a go at it. And rugby union too. Rugby union at the local club on Saturdays. Rugby league on Sunday. And mixed up with that I played two years of Aussie rules as well. There was also soccer thrown in somewhere. I just loved sport, and Queanbeyan High School gave me plenty of opportunity to indulge in it. But mainly it was rugby league until, when I was 16, I gave up everything else and played just golf for a year. Some time after that I went along with some mates to watch a 4th grade (4th team) rugby union match and, on a whim, after the game I had a word with the coach and asked him if he wanted a fullback. He did, and that was really the start – modest enough and without any particular aspirations. But for that year of '79, when I left school, I played a season at 4th grade, we won the premiership for that level and I was put straight into 1st grade level in 1980.

Progress was pretty swift from then on;

within two years I was in the 'green and gold' playing a Test against New Zealand. The first step was ACT U–21, but with a small rugby following in a tiny state that was no major achievement. It happened though at a time when sport was the main thing in my life. I had left school in the 5th form with no particular plans, I was no great shakes at academic studies, and the thing I enjoyed most, really, was playing cricket. I picked up temporary work with no career in mind, and pursued sport with a vigour others would reserve for business careers. I continued with rugby whilst working for a year, and was then selected for a tour to New Zealand with the ACT senior side. Two weeks later I was in the Australian U–21 side. A year on, at age 19, I was brought into the Wallabies party for the New Zealand tour, and won my first cap in the First Test.

In the meantime I had quit my first job. The Queanbeyan rugby union club then took me on as a trainee manager, which is not as spurious an occupation as it sounds. Although rugby clubs in the UK are coming round to it now, in Australia rugby clubs are very much more the social centres of the community, with full facilities, restaurants, bars, games rooms, and so on in use throughout the week. They were, of course, entirely understanding about time off on rugby duty, and there was plenty of that over the succeeding couple of years, before I moved to Sydney. That was prompted by a job opportunity with Wormold International, manufacturers of fire-hydrants, smoke detectors and suchlike, a company with which the present Australian coach Bob Dwyer was involved. It was great, a good wage; I enjoyed Sydney, and I took up with the Randwick club.

By this time rugby had really taken prime position. There were tours to Italy and France in '83, and in that one year I played Tests against the US, Argentina (twice), New Zealand, Italy and France (twice), before the great Fiji and Grand Slam British Isles tour of '84. That has to be the best of all Wallaby touring sides. There was the important element of experienced players like Andy Slack, Roger Gould, Steve Williams, Simon Poidevin, Mark Ella and Brendan Moon, who'd all been to the UK in '81/'82 and knew what was required. Alongside them the new breed; Lynagh, Farr-Jones, Tom Lawton, Tuynman, myself, all 22 or under, with key older recruits in Andy McIntyre and Steve Cutler. Australia had seemed in the past to produce plenty of backs. This time we had the pack to win the forward battle and give us plenty of possession to indulge ourselves in being creative and adventurous.

Rugby was by now well and truly in the blood and I was only too happy to follow in the footsteps of Roger Gould to Petrarca. He had played 'off-season' rugby there in '82 and '83, and when he was unable to go in '84, their coach, Victorio Monari, whom I had met in Australia with Roger, invited me instead, and I went. I was spurred on by the fact that I have relatives in Italy, I had 'hot feet' and wanted to continue seeing as much of the world as I could; I wasn't tied down at home on any front, and you've got to take the chances when they come. Italian rugby is fun, though despite having plenty of good individuals, they've still not really learnt how to combine well. They are slowly learning. Great guys, too, as anywhere in the world in rugby, but when it comes to the football field their mentality isn't always suited to success. It must be that Latin temperament. The game is well-funded there; I think they were ahead of other countries in getting sponsorship in a big way at club level.

I have continued to play there for four seasons now, most recently with Milano. I am well looked after, without being paid for playing, but they give me temporary employment, with accommodation, helping with promotional jobs, and I do my bit for the club on a voluntary basis, working with and organising their junior players.

At home I have had a series of temporary jobs and currently am doing a three-month stint helping to promote Tauranga (Sydney), and Western Plains (Dubbo) Zoos. Believe it or not, I quite like the lions! It's the unconventional nature of my working life that has prompted the snide allegations about being a professional but I've nothing to hide. When I'm on tour I save up the daily allowance and keep it to spend as I choose, and I don't think there are any rules to bar that either.

Not surprisingly, though, I do get irritated by this continuing hassle over rugby's amateur regulations and the 'amateur' way in which the game is run. Considering the money that is coming into the game and the fact that it is the players who provide the spectacle that people, television and sponsors are interested in, there is a simple solution that would satisfy the growing demands of players. When you have a Test match a proportion of the gate-takings may be three or five per cent, whatever is decided, should be withheld and put into a trust fund for the players, which they may only receive when they have quit the game. So when your playing days are over, then according to how many Tests you have played, so you are given the appropriate sum, in proportion to those appearances. In this day and age you cannot apply the same rules that existed 50 years ago. Do we want an increasing number of good players to turn to rugby league? No one is asking for direct payments for turning out on the paddock, but will the game be changed by providing some financial reward to players when they retire? We hear these grand pronouncements from administrators about the 'amateur ethos', yet I see people from the rugby union hierarchies pitch up all over the world at matches, during tours, at the World Cup. Does anyone publish the expenses in detail that they get given? Are their visits, and their expenses always justifiable? You tell me! It's become increasingly clear, especially here in Australia, that if you want to keep top players in the game, you have got to look after them. I find it strange that in New Zealand, by contrast, no one turns to league; I wonder why? Last year, Australia lost three Test players; from what I can gather there's a growing number changing codes in Wales. The incentives become greater as the economic stresses in life increase. I don't blame a guy for switching. I happen to love rugby union; I love seeing the world; I've made many friends. I've no regrets.

I get frustrated, too, about the position that rugby authorities have taken over South Africa. I am a rugby player; I'll play anywhere. Last year I was two days away from a tour of South Africa before it was called off. I read the papers to find out that I might be invited this year. But at this rate I might be 40 before the invitation comes and I get to play. I did make one Sevens tournament, that's all. They are rugby players, so am I; whose opinions should be needed in arriving at a decision on this issue? Politics, to me, stinks. The sooner they get politics out of sport, the better.

I can grouse, too, about the way rugby union is promoted – or not promoted – out here. The popularity here of league and Aussie rules has been helped enormously by cultivating a public interest – games which have such a limited international arena to exploit. But, by contrast, and for example, we had a Test match against British Isles in Sydney this winter, and two of our major TV channels gave no more than the result. The same for the match in Brisbane – where they struggled to get more then 20,000 spectators.

The other football sports promote and advertise – even Tina Turner was used for a major TV commercial. You'll not see a rugby union ad. The papers give 10 times the coverage to league or 'rules'. Who's pulling the strings? Who's cultivating the public interest? Who's pushing the best sport in the world? Someone's stuffing it up, somewhere. You've got to sell in the marketplace. Broaden the interest. It might mean a highly promoted Test match in Melbourne – perhaps Australia v New Zealand; there are a lot of Kiwis there. It might mean a World XV tour to take the game around the country with a well-organised promotion bandwagon rolling in front of it.

So what's in store? I am enjoying my rugby; well, I was until I threw the ball in haste behind Greg Martin in the third British Isles Test! I suppose my enthusiasm was re-kindled when I switched to Randwick, with Bob Dwyer as coach, who then took over from Alan Jones as national coach after the World Cup. Jones did a great job on the Grand Slam tour, there's no denying that, but subsequently he became too dictatorial and we fell out. I got fed up with being verbally lambasted by him, even when we won. After a while you can do without that. Players need freedom to play the game, to make decisions as they see them on the field, and of course, sometimes the gambles don't pay off. Dwyer was more sympathetic and didn't try to get to you to play by numbers. The clash with Jones became inevitable.

I have pondered, like any sane person, tempting approaches from rugby league – St Helen's have been in the forefront of offers from the UK – but I suppose my first objective, presuming selection, would be to pass Simon Poidevin's record caps mark. I don't know. As with, say, Alan Border and Greg Norman, you get some big 'downs' amongst the 'ups'. The press build you up, get you to the top, call you the 'hero'. A week later they call you 'rubbish'. They are like that. The public, too. I remember my first game in Sydney — Randwick versus Warringah. We lost. I don't hang around after the game because there are always so many 'baggers' (ear-bashers, I think, is the English term) to collar you. As I was walking out, and I hadn't played too badly, this guy, a Warringah supporter, presented himself to me and said: "Don't play like that against the Lions, will you!" What can you say to that – nothing. If you win and you play well everyone wants to know you, pat you on the back. Next week, they'll crucify you.

So what's this rugby enjoyment all about? Despite all the gripes it's still the game. I go back to when I was a kid, playing rugby league. I was never the greatest tackler and defender, I was pretty skinny as a youngster. I was fullback – attack good, defence hopeless. I was 'bagged' so many times about defence. There was a very critical attitude amongst players to each other generally, there was a lot of drinking. It wasn't a great social scene. So I went to play union. I was allowed to be a free agent, to be creative. I was young, and wanted to express myself. Looking back it's like yesterday when I played my first Test at 19. Things happened so fast. I remember watching Mark Ella, Glen Ella, Roger Gould, great players, in action against New Zealand in the Bledisloe Cup in 1980. Two years later I was in beside them. I played and listened. Nowadays, is it the same though? I don't see myself as a 'senior citizen' in a side – there are plenty older than me – but when a player has something to say it's good to be listened to. But, nowadays, it's not like that. Young guys, new players, will fire back at you, maybe take offence at you daring to criticise. They know better. So when you play and something goes wrong you try to help, pass comment, and no one listens. One way or another, it shouldn't have been difficult to beat the Lions, given the limitations to the game they played. What was Ieuan Evan's rôle beyond being told to mark and tackle me? There seem to be too many negative influences in the game and too little adventure. We don't encourage flair. Perhaps the increasing emphasis on the forward battle is going to make it a harder, tougher game still. Mind you, the 'brutality' seems to get exaggerated.

Wing, fullback or five-eighth (as in Italy), I guess I'll carry on. In theory, you should be able to play till you're 35 – that seems a hell of a long way off. I'm open-minded. I don't even know whether I'll make myself available for the 1990 tour of New Zealand – I might stay on, after a winter in Italy, enjoy a Mediterranean summer, and remain in the Northern Hemisphere, hopefully to take part in the World Cup.

For now it's off to the zoo! Hopefully I can learn something, so that when I get around to working on a permanent basis it will come as a result of a chance meeting with me as the Tauranga Zoo promotions man. "Oh, yes!", he'll say, "I remember you. How about working for us!"

So, at the time of writing, David Campese remains as a star attraction within the rugby union game, a man vilified by Australia's press and public for having cost the Wallabies the Test series in '89. The wound is deep and may never fully heal, but one hopes he will have learned by now to treat the rugby journalists on his own patch with the contempt they deserve. Nevertheless, the temptation to reconsider the near £300,000 offer from St Helen's rugby league club, that he rejected shortly after the third Lions' Test, must be strong indeed.

David Campese in full flight for the Anzacs as he recovers his form.

THE THIRD TEST
by IAN ROBERTSON

The day after the Second Test the Lions set off from Brisbane along the Gold Coast to Surfers Paradise where they were able to swap their rugby kit for a bucket and spade as they enjoyed a couple of free days in this famous seaside resort. From their hotel close to the magnificent beach, as they watched surfers battle with the crashing waves, the Lions were able to unwind in idyllic surroundings and reflect on a very satisfactory week's work.

From looking down and out after the First Test in Sydney they had turned that form upside down and inside out in Brisbane and they now had a whole week without another match until the decisive Test back in Sydney. I doubt the players could actually have performed a King Canute and stopped the tide, or even the surf, encroaching any further on to the golden sands but at least they had shown that minor miracles were well within their range.

The early part of the week was full of Australian media hype with accusations in every paper every day about the Lions' rough-house tactics. But in the middle of this cauldron of passion, emotion and invective, the Lions' coaches, Ian McGeechan and Roger Uttley, were unmoved. They did not condone the trouble in the first half at Brisbane, but they pointed out that once the game had settled down, the last part of the first half and the whole second half had passed off without any problems. They concluded that the threats of open warfare which had come from the Australian captain, Nick Farr-Jones, as he looked ahead to the Third Test were most unlikely to materialise and would certainly not be prompted by the Lions. Even a rather intimidatory press release from the Australian Rugby Union on the eve of the final Test did not have any adverse effect on the Lions. It read:-

At a Council meeting held today at the Union Headquarters at Kingsford, the Australian Rugby Football Union (ARFU) resolved the following:

1.   To condemn violence in the game.

2.   That the Executive Director prepare a video depicting certain incidents which occurred during the Second Test at Ballymore, which were believed to be prejudicial to the best interests of the game. The video, when prepared, will be forwarded to the Committee of Home Unions for their information and for any action which may be deemed to be appropriate.

3.   The ARFU delegates to International Rugby Football Board (IRFB), have been requested to raise the matter of video evidence as part of the game's judicial system.

Signed

R.J.FORDHAM

Executive Director

This somewhat inflammatory gesture by its very timing was presumably intended to remind the Lions of their moral obligations to respect the image of rugby, especially when any outbreak of violence would be portrayed to a massive worldwide television audience, but I am absolutely convinced that thoughts of a rough match in Sydney were a million miles from Ian McGeechan's mind.

He and the Australian assistant coach, Bob Templeton, settled any lingering doubts I held when I had dinner with both of them two nights before the Third Test. They both agreed that it was impossible to wage war and play good rugby and there was no doubt that the team playing the better rugby would win the series. "Tempo", for so long one of the great figures not only in Australian but also in world rugby, was adamant there would be no trouble in the deciding Test, and it was encouraging to hear two of the game's outstanding coaches join together in condemning the press war of words which surrounded the build-up to this crucial match.

In his short time in charge of Scotland, Ian McGeechan has quickly shown himself to be a coach of the very highest quality and I make absolutely no apology for mentioning him in the same breath as the late Carwyn James. I accept that the style of the Lions' victories throughout the tour fell short of the impeccably high standards set by Carwyn, but these two dedicated rugby intellectuals shared the same ideal. Carwyn James succeeded totally; Ian McGeechan was not quite as successful, yet they journeyed along the same road. Both went out of their way to treat the Lions' party as one unit and not as a mixture of four countries. They each went out of their way to ensure the Lions were a happy united bunch of players who would enjoy the country they were travelling in as well as the rugby. Each player was treated as an individual and made to feel important. As coaches, they worked with and not against the media. They each had a plan of campaign and spent hours devoting themselves to getting the best out of their players. Carwyn enjoyed the benefit of a longer tour and more talented players in 1971 and he achieved more, but Ian McGeechan can be well satisfied with his results. He was painstakingly meticulous every evening in preparing a detailed schedule of everything they would try to do in the following day's two-hour training session and in this he had tremendous assistance from Roger Uttley.

I feel that Carwyn James, alone of British coaches in the last two decades, would have achieved more than McGeechan and Uttley did and that is because I believe he had the genius to weave his magic a little more quickly. I believe he would have got the British Lions' backs firing early on in the tour by encouraging them to take risks, and consequently, by the time of the Tests, they would have developed the confidence to play expansive rugby.

Having said that, McGeechan and Uttley worked wonders to guide the Lions from the disaster of the First Test to the supreme triumph of the Third Test. I would dare to suggest that if these two coaches had had the Lions for another few weeks after the final Test they would have further developed their talents to such an extent that they would have had a good chance of beating the All Blacks.

As it was, they turned the tour into a triumph by winning the Third Test. If there were too many mistakes made by both sides to make this game a classic, at least it was thrilling and rivetting and in doubt right up to the final whistle. The forwards succeeded in doing a partial demolition job on the Wallaby pack and that helped the Lions keep their opponents in a vice-like grip under intense pressure throughout the game.

However, for all the heroics of every single Lion, three players stood out above all others – Finlay Calder, Dean Richards and Mike Teague were the real match-winners. They launched the punitive series of driving rucks and mauls which eventually broke the Australian resistance; they were quicker to almost every breakdown and they were generally faster than their opponents in thought and action all afternoon. They helped to establish a forward superiority which finally overwhelmed the Wallabies.

They could not have achieved this if Ackford and Dooley had not had the edge at the line-out, and if the scrummage had not been so immovable, and full credit must go to the whole pack. Behind this marvellous platform Robert Jones and Rob Andrew again played well together introducing more variety in attack and the same tenacious tackling in defence which made them seem at times like two extra loose-forwards. Just like shoes, scissors and spectacles, half-backs are best when they come in pairs and it was a great comfort for the Lions that Jones and Andrew gelled so well considering that these two Tests in Austalia were the first two games they had ever played together.

Apart from the occasional weak kick, they hardly made a mistake between them in 160 minutes of Test rugby and that gave the forwards in front of them enormous confidence. The tackling of the whole back division was quite breathtaking, especially in the second half when the Wallabies staged their dramatic recovery, but two players were exceptional and deserve special mention. Scott Hastings rattled in several priceless tackles to save potentially dangerous situations, and the fact that David Campese was virtually blotted out of all three Tests reflects huge credit on Ieuan Evans.

Rory Underwood and Jerry Guscott were a neat mix of bustling defence and fast support play and Gavin Hastings was at his very best at fullback. He was faultless in defence, caught everything which was hoisted in his direction and he remained a menacing threat in attack.

A tug-of-war for rival wings Ieuan Evans and Ian Williams.

Finlay Calder at the feet of Nick Farr-Jones, but Calder was on top of the world at the final whistle.

Never has one point meant so much – the Lions celebrate their narrow victory.

Euphoria ....

.... followed by exhaustion.

He also kicked five penalty goals from seven attempts and that was an average not even Michael Lynagh could better. The Lions' try was a fortunate affair because it owed more to an error of judgement on the part of David Campese than any cunning on the part of the Lions, although it must be stressed the furious following up of Evans played a significant role. A drop goal from Andrew flew wide and Campese decided to open out from behind his own goal-line. No sooner had he crossed into the field of play than he was confronted by Evans breathing fire and fury. Campese threw the ball at his fullback, Greg Martin, but he dropped a difficult pass and Evans pounced

It was sad to see such a great player give away such a soft try but it was also ridiculous for the press, especially the Australian press, to destroy him so unmercifully for stepping down from his exalted pedestal for one brief unfortunate moment. The press blamed only Campo for the Test defeat; not the fact that their pack were destroyed, not the very poor quality of their kicking, not the fact that their breakaway forwards were wiped out in the loose, nor the fact that they lacked strike power in midfield. These were the real reasons why the Wallabies lost and if five Australians had not given away five penalties which cost Australia 15 points, then the Wallabies would have won 18–4

Lynagh kicked four penalties and converted a try by Ian Williams. At half-time the score was 9–9. Three minutes into the second half Lynagh gave Australia a 12–9 lead only for Evans to score his try three minutes later. Midway through the half Gavin Hastings kicked two penalties in the space of two minutes to open up a seven point lead. It seemed all over. It wasn't.

The Wallabies, competitors to their last breath, fought back magnificently and Lynagh landed two penalties. 19–18. Eight minutes left. It was a fabulous finale as the Australians bravely threw everything into attack even from their own line and the Lions defended the bridge like fifteen latterday Horatios. It was desperate, pulsating, unforgettable rugby. The Test series and the immediate future of British and Australian rugby depended on it. The Lions held out; the Wallabies failed heroically.

After all that had happened the previous week, the image of rugby was restored in all its glory as there was not a single unsavoury incident worth a mention and that, perhaps, was the most appropriate epitaph. The tingling excitement of the last quarter of an hour overshadowed everything else on the tour and the scenes at the end will remain etched in the minds of the Lions for ever. The packed partisan crowd were baying for Australia. It suddenly seemed possible they could achieve the impossible. Eventually the final whistle went and it was all over. The Lions were so emotionally overcome, they did a lap of honour, hitherto unheard of in international rugby.

Against all the odds after the First Test the Lions had clinched the series and made a little piece of history. For the first time ever the Lions had lost an opening Test and recovered to win a series. The message at the end of six hard weeks was simple – mission accomplished.

Postscript

July 15th 1989 will go down as a great day for British rugby, for captain Finlay Calder, and for his old school Daniel Stewart's in Edinburgh. There was Calder, a Daniel in the Lions' den. More encouraging news was to follow. Another former pupil of Daniel Stewart's, the Right Reverend William MacDonald, had been chosen as the new Moderator of the General Assembly of the Church of Scotland. It seemed a remarkable coincidence to discover that one small Scottish school should in the same year produce both the leader of the Christians and the leader of the Lions. How could such a dynamic combination lose a Test series. They couldn't. It was no surprise, then, that these 1989 Lions could, as Calder put it, "come back from the dead like Lazarus" following the First Test humiliation. In Brisbane and the return visit to Sydney, they produced two miracles. And, the Heavens be praised, at the Sydney Football Stadium in the Third Test, they won in style, playing their best rugby of the tour. The final message from Sydney was written loud and clear in tablets of stone – British rugby, so long in the wilderness, was back in business. Hallelujah!

The policemen's lot on this occasion was a very happy one.

AN INTERVIEW WITH IAN McGEECHAN

After the Third Test

IAN ROBERTSON Do you think the Lions' performance in the Third Test was their best of the tour?

IAN McGEECHAN Yes, it was far and away our best performance because not only did we get it right tactically, the execution of those tactics showed tremendous discipline and control and the slight change of emphasis in our play caught the Australians on the hop and gave us the initiative.

IAN ROBERTSON Can you summarise your tactical blueprint for success?

IAN McGEECHAN We had been very static in the scrum and line-out in the First Test and we had almost beaten ourselves before we started. We were much more positive and dynamic in the Second Test and we developed this driving forward play one stage further in the Third Test. Our scrum was rock solid and we were able to vary our game much more than the Wallabies who were under far more pressure in the set scrums. This gave us a key advantage. While they had great difficulty from scrums in doing anything other than passing the ball to Michael Lynagh which limited their attacking permutations and made our defence relatively easy, we had plenty of options. Dean Richards could and did break, and so did Mike Teague, and so did Finlay Calder, and the momentum of our dominant set scrum meant each of these players could cross the gain line before being tackled. With the three loose-forwards, all outstanding support players, we were well able to make sizeable dents in the opposition, gain valuable ground, tie in their breakaway players before presenting our half-backs with great loose-ball going forward. On other occasions Robert Jones had the option from this wonderful scrummage possession to break himself, to kick or to pass. And similarly, at fly-half, Rob Andrew was able to dictate and control the course of the match. It was exactly the same at the line-out and in the loose. In the First Test we won a line-out and simply fed Robert Jones. In the Second Test, we regularly caught the ball and drove forward through the middle of the line-out to give the backs better possession. In the Third Test, the Wallabies expected this, but we had then changed the direction of our attack. We drove round the front and through the back with Dean Richards and David Sole, the key men, as well as for variety also occasionally driving through the middle. The point is that the Australians were never quite sure what we were going to do with our scrum or line-out possession and that put us firmly in the driving seat. We quite deliberately kept shifting the target and that kept the Wallabies guessing and in two minds all the time. This set-piece domination and, most important of all, the varied way in which we used it enabled us to win about three times as much second phase possession and we were in control of the game.

IAN ROBERTSON What pleased you most about the Lions' pack in the Third Test?

IAN McGEECHAN I think I would have to say our play in the open. It began to click in the last 20 minutes of the Second Test, but it was even more dynamic and controlled and precise in the Third Test. The ball carrier often knocked opponents backwards and the support play was the best of the whole tour. Equally significant, the presentation of the ball from the carrier to the

Ian McGeechan plots Australia's downfall with captain Finlay Calder and man-of-the-series Mike Teague.

first man up in support was the best we had seen and that was no coincidence because we had spent ages trying to perfect this art. I was delighted with the close-quarter handling and running of the forwards which was quicker, slicker and far more abrasively positive than anything earlier in the tour. Again, by setting up and winning rucks and mauls and driving powerfully forward we kept our options open. Sometimes we could give the backs quick ball and other times the last forward to the breakdown could pick the ball up and drive forward himself to make further inroads into the Australian defence and stretch it to its limits. I was delighted with our power in the loose. At last the pack were thundering forward in the open with their bodies low in excellent driving positions and their legs pumping away in double quick time. The way the pack rocketed Dan Crowley and the Wallaby pack 25 yards backwards in the Second Test in one fierce furious offensive highlighted the growing gap between the two packs by the end of the series. But you have to remember this outstanding rucking and mauling can't happen overnight and it was the end result of six weeks intensive effort and countless hours of practice.

IAN ROBERTSON If the forwards were the architects of the victory in the last two Tests, how big a role did the backs play?

IAN McGEECHAN The backs did everything that was asked of them and if they hadn't we would have lost the series. Firstly, they created the two tries at the end of the Second Test which kept the series alive. Secondly, they played a crucial role in our plan to keep shifting the target area in the Third Test, when we played our most expansive rugby of the series and they had the confidence to do this. Thirdly, the tackling of the backs was absolutely fantastic throughout the whole of the Second and Third Tests with just one lapse in 160 minutes which allowed Lynagh to create the try for Ian Williams. The way Robert Jones policed Nick Farr-Jones, and Ieuan Evans stuck to Campese, and Scott Hastings and Rob Andrew tackled everything in sight, was fantastic; the collective defensive effort of the backs was of paramount importance. Fourthly, the tactical kicking and general decision making of our half-backs, Jones and Andrew, were quite outstanding and perfectly complemented the heroics of the forwards. They fully exploited the advantage which the pack had seized and that was no mean achievement. When you consider that the Australian half-backs, Lynagh and Farr-Jones, have played together for five full seasons, while Jones and Andrew were playing together for the first time in the Brisbane Test and the second time in Sydney, you have some measure of the enormity of their achievement. Individually they had each shown a tremendous amount of footballing talent for Wales and England but I reckon collectively as a half-back partnership they made more good decisions during the last two Tests than they've ever made before in a whole season of international rugby in Britain. And remember, they made all these cool tactical decisions in the most highly charged and emotional atmosphere imaginable – Test match rugby for the British Lions when they were already one Test down in a three Test series. They were calling the right shots, by and large, for 160 minutes of pressurised, claustrophobic rugby and I think they'll both go on to even better things after this tour.

IAN ROBERTSON How much did the Lions improve between the First and Third Tests?

IAN McGEECHAN We improved out of all recognition in so many different areas. Our whole attitude, our mental approach was totally transformed after the First Test for the next two Tests. Technically we improved dramatically in our driving forward play and the use we made of our possession, and tactically we moved up a couple of notches. The overall quality of our play was perhaps 50 per cent better by the time we returned to Sydney for the Third Test and perhaps the most interesting fact of all is that I believe this Test team still had not reached its full potential, and given another three weeks together would have been very much better. By then the pack would have been almost unstoppable and I believe the backs would have been ready to join in an expansive game of running rugby. We had hoped to achieve this midway through the tour but it just didn't work out in our favour.

IAN ROBERTSON Why do you think we saw so little good back play during the tour, considering the formidable play of the forwards almost from the very first match in Perth?

IAN McGEECHAN The simple answer to a complex question is that it is much easier to drill a pack of forwards than create brilliant back play. With tremendous help from Roger Uttley, who did a magnificent job, we achieved most of what we set out to do with the forwards by the end of the tour but I can't say the same for the backs. I concentrated on the lines of running, on speed of passing, on alignment and angles of attack rather than working on a series of set moves, and a great deal of progress was made, but just not quickly enough, especially when the whole team failed to fire in the First Test which meant we weren't in a position to take wholesale risks in the Second Test. It wasn't then the time to start bold experimenting in the Third Test.

IAN ROBERTSON What were your biggest disappointments during the six weeks in Australia?

IAN McGEECHAN The biggest disappointment was obviously our lack-lustre performance in the First Test closely followed by the failure of the backs to really sparkle in the Test series. My only other major disappointment was the reaction or rather over-reaction by the media to the controversial incidents in the first half of the Second Test. I would never condone dangerous play, indeed I would always condemn it, and the Lions' management did admonish players for overstepping the mark. I explained to the team that it was possible to be physically very aggressive within the laws of the game and there was never any need to resort to unsavoury tactics.

IAN ROBERTSON What do you feel was the great strength of the 1989 British Lions?

IAN McGEECHAN I would say the unity of the group. They were an extremely happy party who were all prepared to work hard towards the same goal. There were no factions and when we lost the First Test we were able to close ranks, work even closer together, look at ourselves honestly and critically and begin to rebuild our whole structure. Furthermore, we did this as the Lions and not as England, Scotland, Ireland and Wales. Roger Uttley and I looked at the strengths of the 30 players at our disposal and based all our plans on their particular talents rather than trying to force a group of players to change their ways and adapt to say, for example, the Scottish way of rucking or the English style of mauling.

IAN ROBERTSON You and Roger Uttley were both members of the unbeaten 1974 Lions. They were generally regarded as a team of great forwards and good backs. Would it be fair to describe the 1989 Lions in the same way?

IAN McGEECHAN Yes, I suppose that is how people will look back on this tour although I am convinced the backs had it in them to play really well at the very highest level. I certainly believe the pack would give the current All Blacks team a real run for their money and I don't believe there is such a big gulf between the Northern Hemisphere countries and Australia and New Zealand. If we didn't ask our leading players to play a ridiculous number of matches, hoping they could peak 50 or 60 times a year, and went for quality rather than quantity, I believe we would get very close to All Black standards. They are the best in the world and we must strive to reach their standards. I honestly don't think we are that far behind and given the right domestic circumstances I reckon we could close the gap completely.

IAN ROBERTSON I know it's a leading and divisive question, but which players would you say were the key players in the Lions Test team?

IAN McGEECHAN David Sole would be one for his contribution in the scrum, as a support player in the line-out and as a human dynamo in the loose. Wade Dooley for his efforts in the last two Tests. The whole back row, but especially Mike Teague and Dean Richards. In the backs, I would pick out Robert Jones and Ieuan Evans but I must add, victory in the Tests was a real team effort and the success of the tour was shared by the whole party of 35 and that includes the doctor, Ben Gilfeather, and the physio, Kevin Murphy, who kept disruption from injury down to the very barest minimum.

IAN ROBERTSON Who would you name as the three players who made the most progress in the six weeks of the tour?

IAN McGEECHAN Strictly in playing terms I would choose Jerry Guscott and Mike Griffiths. And from a tactical point of view I think Rob Andrew will return a more complete fly-half.

IAN ROBERTSON As you prepared a tactical analysis for each Test who did you feel were the key Australian players?

IAN McGEECHAN Lynagh, Farr-Jones, Walker, Miller and Cutler, and we made our plans accordingly. For example, with our pack on top and Farr-Jones under pressure, instead of Robert Jones dropping back to cover the box on their ball, he stayed up on the offside line to harry and hassle Farr-Jones. We tried to do this sort of thing to all of their key men.

IAN ROBERTSON What has the first Lions victory in a Test series since 1974 done for British rugby?

IAN McGEECHAN I think it has shown that once again we can compete at the top level and we should have the confidence to go on from here and continue this development. If we restructure the game in Britain, as I have already said, and make less demands on our leading players, we could look forward even more optimistically to the 1991 World Cup. But we have taken a big step forward this summer and made a lot of progress. I think we can be proud of what the Lions achieved and build on this success next season.

IAN ROBERTSON Finally, if you could choose just one highlight from the whole tour what would it be?

IAN McGEECHAN It would have to be the final few minutes of the Second Test in which we scored two tries, saved the series and gave credibility to British rugby. I could have said the final whistle in the Third Test, but that would have meant nothing if it hadn't been for that purple passage in the Second Test.

THE ANZACS MATCH
AND TOUR EPITAPH
by IAN ROBERTSON

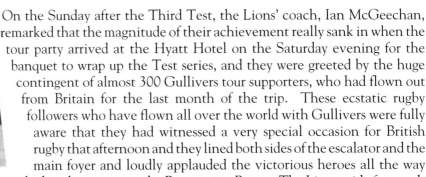

On the Sunday after the Third Test, the Lions' coach, Ian McGeechan, remarked that the magnitude of their achievement really sank in when the tour party arrived at the Hyatt Hotel on the Saturday evening for the banquet to wrap up the Test series, and they were greeted by the huge contingent of almost 300 Gullivers tour supporters, who had flown out from Britain for the last month of the trip. These ecstatic rugby followers who have flown all over the world with Gullivers were fully aware that they had witnessed a very special occasion for British rugby that afternoon and they lined both sides of the escalator and the main foyer and loudly applauded the victorious heroes all the way from the hotel entrance to the Banqueting Room. The Lions said afterwards it was probably the most moving moment of the whole tour. If the Lions had been regarded as men of Lilliput after the First Test, they were surely more like the giants of Brobdingnag after the Third Test. Like the original Gulliver they had travelled a long way in a relatively short time.

Warm tributes have been paid already to the coaches and players in the Lions' party as well as to all the considerable efforts of the back room staff, especially the two medical men, but it would be an awful omission if mention were not made of the tour manager, Clive Rowlands. He emerged from the trials and tribulations of the six weeks in Australia with his formidable reputation not only unscathed but actually enhanced.

He was a very important guiding influence for the players and he was an extremely popular manager with the Lions' party. In talking to half-a-dozen players at the end of the tour they were united in voting Clive one of the best tour managers they had ever travelled with, and there is no doubt he worked tirelessly from the first day to the last day on behalf of his family of 35, putting their interests first and foremost at all times. He was admirably suited to playing the role of the good shepherd to his flock and, by concentrating on all the administrative and organisational duties so efficiently, he took a huge weight of responsibility off the shoulders of Ian McGeechan and Roger Uttley.

He decided very wisely not to interfere too much on the playing side leaving that almost exclusively to his two extremely capable coaches. Having said that, he did, in the first fortnight of the tour, spend some time showing the scrum-halves how to kick to the box. After he had put up two towering kicks, Ian McGeechan, haunted like every Scotsman by the 111 line-outs Rowlands orchestrated for Wales at Murrayfield in 1967, exclaimed, "Just another 109 to go, I suppose, Clive".

Articulate at the after-match functions and fiercely loyal to the Lions' cause, he ended the tour as one of the best Lions' managers of the past quarter of a century, right up there alongside Doug Smith and Syd Millar. If there was any hint of criticism lobbed in his direction it might be that he was not always gushingly forthcoming at press conferences but he was certainly very fair and proved as helpful and co-operative as a Lions manager is expected to be. He once or twice ended press conferences rather abruptly, but that was partly because he didn't suffer fools gladly and with a retinue of over 50 media men following the tour, including a dozen who can best be described as pretty lightweight, it was not a bad fault to have.

One of his easiest press conferences followed the huge win over the New South Wales country side in Newcastle in the penultimate match of the trip.

Midweek captain Donal Lenihan with his team T-shirt.

The Lions scored 14 tries to 1 and by scoring 72 points they were only 27 points short of the Lions' record total achieved in 1974 against South Western Districts at Mossel Bay in South Africa. However, the real significance of that victory was not the huge score so much as the fact that the midweek side, captained by Donal Lenihan and known affectionately as 'Donal's Doughnuts', had finished the tour unbeaten, unlike their more illustrious Saturday side.

In recognition of their excellent results, the midweek team gained their just desserts when six of them were promoted to the 'senior' side for the final match against the Anzacs in Brisbane. The Lions' management stressed that they did not regard this game as a fourth Test and they had not picked their strongest side. A few who had been on the fringe of the Test side were being given their chance of glory in a big match. The midweek midfield trio were selected *en bloc* with the inclusion of Chalmers, Mullin and Devereux and with Scott Hastings switching to the left wing. In the pack, Bob Norster and Andy Robinson were chosen initially and when Dean Richards dropped out with an injured shoulder, Derek White was also promoted.

The concept of an Anzac team was welcomed in Britain, Australia and New Zealand when it was first announced but, sadly, by the time the match was due to be played many months later, the whole idea had fallen apart; the whole dream wrecked by internal shenanigans in New Zealand. Admittedly the timing was not perfect. The match was played a week after the All Blacks First Test and a week before their Second Test against Argentina. Furthermore, the New Zealand international against Australia for the Bledisloe Cup was due to be played two weeks after the Anzacs game.

But that is still no real excuse for so many All Blacks declining the invitation and dropping out at late notice. In the fortnight beforehand 12 All Blacks dropped out – a handful through injury but the vast majority because they just didn't want to play. The New Zealand Rugby Union, who had been party to the whole concept, simply opted out of their responsibility. They stood by and did nothing. This was an insult to the Australians and an insult to the British Lions.

If the New Zealand Rugby Union had told their players that if they refused to represent New Zealand in the Anzac side, which was unquestionably within their amateur rights, the Union would respect that attitude, but would almost certainly not bother to ask them to play for the All Blacks for the next three years. Had that been the case, I have a hunch those players might well have changed their minds. I believe the players and the New Zealand Union got their priorities wrong and embarrassed Australia and the Lions. In the event the match was robbed of the presence of John Gallagher, John Kirwan, Terry Wright, Bernie McCahill, Joe Stanley, John Schuster, Richard Loe, Gary Whetton, Alan Whetton, Zinzan Brooke, Mike Brewer and Wayne Shelford.

Of the three All Blacks who did turn up, although Frano Botica and Kieran Crowley had played for New Zealand, only the prop, Steve McDowell, was an established current All Black. The feeling of anti-climax which surrounded this match was hard to avoid but it still took another remarkable act of escapology from the Lions to produce their 11th win on the 12-match tour.

Just as in the First Test, the forwards failed to fire on all cylinders and they were out-played in the line-out and in the loose. They were only level 6–6 at half-time by dint of a spectacular individual try by Brendan Mullin in injury time, after spending most of the first half defending, albeit superbly. In the

second half, despite a splendid try by Devereux created by the Hastings brothers, and a penalty by Gavin Hastings, the boot of Michael Lynagh and a great try by Ian Williams had put the Anzacs 15–13 ahead with ten minutes remaining.

New Zealand's depleted contribution to the Anzac team: left to right, Botica, McDowell and Crowley.

At this point the Lions looked beyond the pale with three replacements on the field for David Young (injured ribs), BrendanMullin and Ieuan Evans (both dislocated shoulders). The replacements, Mike Griffiths, Rob Andrew and Tony Clement were all playing out of position and the odds seemed stacked against the Lions. This was the final ultimate test for the 1989 British Lions and somehow they managed to dredge the energy from somewhere to stage a supreme rally and perform their famous Houdini trick one more time.

They had had to come from behind in dramatic fashion so often in the big matches, it was almost a way of life for the Lions and it certainly added to the excitement. The pack led the charge and in the space of 90 seconds, right at the end of the game, first Craig Chalmers and then Gavin Hastings dropped goals to snatch victory from a match which seemed to have been lost.

The final whistle went and the tour was over. The second most successful Lions side in history could look back on a job well done.

In a curious way, history repeated itself at Ballymore because the Lions scored 19 points in all three of their matches in Brisbane against Queensland,

Australia and the Anzacs. And there was another curious historical coincidence. On a day when three of the most famous veterans of the old Anzac regiment were presented to the teams before the match, the final scoreline of 19–15 had a haunting, ironic ring about it because 1915 remains the best known date in Anzac history. That was the year, on the orders of the British High Command, that the Anzac troops were sent into battle in the First World War at Gallipoli against the Turks with disastrous consequences and tragic loss of life.

1989 will be remembered not as another bad year for the Anzacs, but as a promising year for British rugby after so long in the doldrums. But it has to be stressed that the Lions had still failed to blossom fully and they had once again, against the Anzacs, promised a little more than they had actually achieved. Nonetheless, they had done very much better than the 1977, 1980 and 1983 Lions. In a final optimistic flush of enthusiasn, the followers of the 1989 Lions felt, as they left Ballymore for the last time, that perhaps the full potential of these Lions might finally be realised in their next game against France in Paris in October. We reckoned it would be certainly well worthwhile crossing the Channel to find out. Meanwhile, we knew for sure it had been well worthwhile crossing the world to Australia in July to watch British rugby regain its credibility and respectability.

Nick Farr-Jones is introduced to Sir Edward 'Weary' Dunlop, one of three Anzac veterans who were guests at Ballymore.

Nick Farr-Jones, the Australian captain – always in the thick of the battle.

Tension shows during the First Test.

Michael Lynagh,
good tactical
kicking and 14
points in the First
Test.

David Campese makes the ball available despite the attention of Robert Jones, Dean Richards and Craig Chalmers.

Heads down as
Finlay Calder leads
his dejected Lions
from the field after
their crushing
defeat at Sydney.

A change of sport
for John Jeffrey and
Gary Armstrong.

Hard work and relaxation for the Lions between matches.

Good protection
from the forwards
as Mike Teague
prepares to feed the
ball to Robert
Jones.

Donal Lenihan, who led the midweek side to morale-boosting wins throughout the tour.

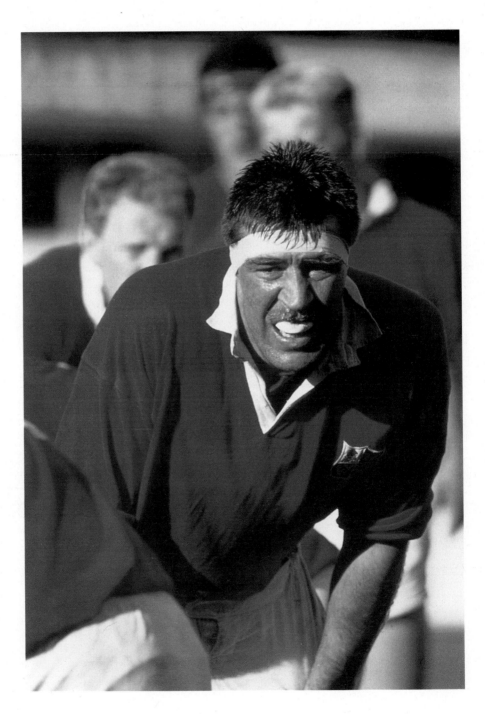

Gary Armstrong
sets up an attack
against New
South Wales 'B' at
Dubbo.

Gareth Chilcott
at full stretch
against New
South Wales
Country XV at
Newcastle.

Another
important training
session.

Finlay Calder leads
from the front in
the critical Third
Test.

Ian Williams's
pace beats Rory
Underwood's dive
to put Australia
level in the Third
Test.

Gavin Hastings adds three more points to the Lions total in the Third Test.

Ieuan Evans beats Greg Martin to the touchdown as the hapless Campese looks on.

The moment of victory as the final whistle blows and the series is won.

Gavin Hastings,
Dean Richards,
Ieuan Evans and
Rory Underwood
celebrate with the
Lions mascot.

WORLDWIDE RUGBY

The French Succession
by CHRIS THAU

The election of the French Federation President, Albert Ferrasse, as President of the 43-nation Federation Internationale de Rugby Amateur, better known as FIRA, was meant to be the first act in the succession saga of French rugby.

The old scenario with Marcel Batigne as supporting cast was re-enacted. In 1968 Batigne, one of the old pals of Ferrasse, stepped down as President of the French Federation to make room for his friend Albert. The El Caudillo from Agen has ruled French rugby with an iron hand ever since, while Batigne was rewarded with the 'life' presidency of FIRA.

In June 1989, Batigne retired on health grounds from the French run international Federation and, miraculously, Ferrasse arrived in Moscow ready to step into his shoes. The 47th FIRA Congress unanimously approved the election of Ferrasse as the supremo of the largest international rugby federation in the world in August 1989; the IRB has 40 members while FIRA has 43.

In the Bonapartist tradition of French rugby, Ferrasse is supposed to step down in 1991, after the World Cup or during 1992, to allow his protégé, the current French coach Jacques Fouroux, to take over and consolidate his power base before the 1993 'Presidential elections'.

Fouroux in turn is supposed to hand over the much-coveted coaching job to his alter-ego and supporter, the French scrum-half and captain, Pierre Berbizier. The whole script has the tired air of an old dynastic transition.

But suddenly the picture does not seem to be as clear as that. While Fouroux, elected vice-president of the French Federation in the spring of 1989, has made known his decision to appoint Berbizier as his heir apparent, Ferrasse spoiled the scenario by introducing the Dubroca factor into the equation.

The 1987 Grand Slam skipper Daniel Dubroca, a farmer in Sainte Bazeille and captain-cum-coach of Ferrasse's beloved Agen, was appointed, at Ferrasse's insistence, Fouroux's assistant coach during the June tour of New Zealand, and has been co-opted onto the French selection panel, to replace Aldo Gruarin.

The value of the shares of the Fouroux-Berbizier cartel seems to have taken a sudden plunge. The informed rumour has it that Fouroux – in his impetuous and highly-charged style – has upset some of Ferrasse's buddies, the *eminence gris* of French rugby, Guy Basquet, in particular.

Basquet, the President of the Agen club and vice-president of the French Federation, had been Ferrasse's captain both at Agen and in the French national team when Ferrasse was on the replacements bench. It is said that the former skipper of Agen until a few years ago, and secretary of the club, Charles Calbet, is even more influential than the former French skipper.

Irrespective of whether the story is true or not, Dubroca's recall from semi-retirement just before the Five Nations game against Scotland was reminiscent of the way Fouroux was extracted out of the near-anonymity of his home-town club of Auch – after his spectacular retirement from international rugby – to be appointed the coach of a French team which had been humiliated 15–0 by the Romanians.

The man responsible for the initial approach then was Guy Basquet, though very few have any doubt that it was Ferrasse who has orchestrated the whole move.

Fouroux's career at the helm was spectacular, though the controversy which has followed his career became embarrassingly strident during the last few years. Within a year of taking over the French team, Fouroux, with Jean Pique as his assistant, delivered an admittedly lucky Grand Slam in 1981.

He disciplined the notoriously rebellious French forwards and with Pierre Romeu as assistant, brought France another Grand Slam in 1987, coaching the 'tricolores' to the final of the first World Cup. However, for bizarre reasons he seemed unable to manage his PR campaign with the same masterly authority he had employed in his professional life and coaching career.

The French media has never forgiven him for being hand-picked by Ferrasse, without substantial club coaching credentials. While his numerous

Fouroux and Berbizier with the French squad.

enemies pointed out that he coached France before he had coached a club, Fouroux, supported by a few, yet influential, friends, maintained that the best coaching experience was to captain France and serve an apprenticeship under 'Monsieur Jean', the flamboyant coach of Grenoble, Jean Lienard, Fouroux's former mentor at La Voulte.

Last June's tour to New Zealand has reinforced Fouroux's belief in the simple virtues of All Black rugby, in what he calls "a collective playing instinct". "We have two seasons to make up for fifty years gap if we want to have the same chance as New Zealand in the World Cup" he said.

He points out, rightly, that the gap between the French and New Zealand players is to be found in what he calls their rugby education and environment. "Our present technical shortcomings simply prevent us from being the best in the world. It is as simple as that", he said after returning from New Zealand. Fouroux's obsession with the All Black supremacy has been criticised, and derided. But it seems obvious that Fouroux's recipe is the key, not necessarily the only one, to the secret vault of New Zealand rugby.

"The 11th commandment of New Zealand rugby is: 'Don't make mistakes'. 'Force the opposition to make mistakes', is the 12th", Fouroux says with glee.

His views are shared by both Berbizier and Dubroca, between them the axel of the 1987 Grand Slam and the dominant figures in the Agen playing set-up. Fouroux had already expressed a desire to distance himself from the nitty-gritty of coaching the French team. He has already delegated a substantial degree of power to Pierre Berbizier. The Agen scrum-half had emerged as Fouroux's potential successor during the 1987 unofficial tour of Scotland, when he coached the side for two days before Fouroux – on a business trip abroad – could join the tourists. During the past Five Nations campaign Fouroux has taken an increasingly laid back position, allowing Berbizier, described by virtually everyone in French rugby as one of the most competent men around, a considerable degree of freedom in preparing the team.

Fouroux, elected vice-president of the French Federation, wants to spend more time on the drawing board in an attempt to give French rugby a sense of direction, an ethos and structure. He has invited some of the foremost coaching minds in French rugby, Pierre Conquet, René Délaplace, Raoul Barrière, Jean Lienard and Robert Bru to join him in producing his master plan for the future. Only Bru, closely associated with the Toulouse club, has turned him down.

Berbizier is also part of this think tank, while Dubroca, recently appointed selector, may also take over temporarily as Fouroux's assistant, should Romeu step down, or be discarded.

It is quite clear that Pierre Villepreux, the brilliant coach of the champion

Berbizier and Dubroca: partners or rivals?

club, Toulouse, has lost the battle so far. But that does not mean he has given up his ambition to coach the French team at some point in the future. His decision to join England during their Portuguese training break has stirred up a hot debate in French rugby and brought the former French fullback in direct conflict with Ferrasse and Co. The Federation has even threatened to ban Villepreux for failing to ask permission to coach the English. The threat seemed to have had an effect on the belligerent Toulouse coaching set-up. But the sharp debate has had a polarising effect of French rugby. Villepreux has emerged as the leader of the 'loyal' opposition. Should Ferrasse and company make a mistake, he, actively supported by his club President, the former French captain Jean Fabré, and other disgruntled club officials and administrators could form an effective, and possibly successful, alliance.

But, with a new group of Ferrasse supporters elected among the top Federation positions at the Bordeaux congress, the succession of Fouroux seems secure.

A VISIT TO HONG KONG
by BILL McLAREN

He was a large, rugged, athletic son of the South Pacific and he put it in a nutshell: "I would call the Hong Kong Sevens the Olympics of Rugby Football". It is a view echoed by virtually everyone who has experienced the magic of that fabulous tournament. Perhaps the one contrast with the Olympics and its unsavoury aspects is that it would be hard to find a rugby event that more encapsulated all the good things that the Rugby Union game has to offer than that extraordinary show-piece seven-a-side international event organised by the Hong Kong RFC with magnificent sponsorship support from Cathay Pacific and the Hong Kong and Shanghai Bank.

The 14th tournament, contested on Saturday and Sunday, April 1 and 2, by 24 teams from all over the rugby firmament, not only attracted capacity audiences of 28,000 on each day but produced a shoal of magnificent tries and superb team play, against a background of fierce competition allied to impeccable sportsmanship and on-field behaviour and thoroughly enjoyable audience participation. In Hong Kong the mighty meet with the midgets so that some pool ties result in runaway victories. Brunei lost to Australia and Bahrain to New Zealand, each by 52–0. Yet just to have played against these two rugby giants represented for the Brunei and Bahrain players a memorable highlight. They never threw in the sponge, and later had the satisfaction of reaching the semi-final of the Bowl championship. Whoever heard of people in Thailand, Sri Lanka, Malaysia and Taipei playing rugby? Yet there they were, proud to represent their countries, immaculately turned out, lacking in most cases physical presence but moving the ball around dextrously and clearly revelling in the distinctive atmosphere. Tunisia were at the Hong Kong Sevens for the very first time and in the matter of on-field discipline they were a credit to the game, an example to all.

One of the many pleasing features of the Hong Kong tournament is that, unlike most sevens in the UK, in which once beaten a side is eliminated, the pool sections at Hong Kong simply decide which of the three teams in each pool will later contest the knock-out stages for the Cup, Plate and Bowl championships. Thus, each team in the tournament is assured of two ties on the Saturday and at least one, and perhaps as many as three, ties on the Sunday. Imagine the elation and sense of achievement experienced by the Netherlands squad. They conceded 40 points in losing both pool matches to the American Eagles and Hong Kong. Yet, in the Bowl on the Sunday, they beat Italy by 8–4 after extra time, Bahrain by 24–4 in the semi-final and then

Far left The Netherlands celebrate their winning try against Spain.
Left Scott Hastings leads the Barbarian recovery against Australia.
Below A green oasis in a concrete jungle.

won the trophy in the first all-European final with victory by 20–16 over Spain after 4 minutes of extra time. Four Marcker brothers, Hans, Andre, Mats and Peter, shared in this triumph, as did their English manager and adviser, Dennis Power, but the player who made the biggest impression was a gangly lad with a head of hair like a wind-blown thatched cottage, Bart Wierenga, who ran his heart out in a series of tingling performances.

Most touching of all was the fact that the Netherlands party included Marcel Bierman, rugby internationalist, cyclist and footballer, who suffered a broken neck in a tackle during the 1988 Hong Kong Sevens and is now confined to a wheelchair.

Marcel's huge smile as he was wheeled by Wierenga alongside his team mates on their lap of honour was one of the enduring memories of a great occasion.

The unfettered joy of the majority of the capacity crowd also was seen and heard at each success of the local Hong Kong seven, who squeezed through by 16–14 against the Netherlands, then brought the house down with a 16–6 winning margin over the American Eagles. It was the first time that Hong Kong had reached the quarter final of the Cup championship and they owed much to the support work of Neil Barclay (a vital score against Netherlands), and Mark Ashall (two tries against the Americans), to the inspired leadership of 6ft 2ins centre Pieter Schats, and to the abrasive approach of their blonde, bumble-bee, Gary Cross, Pink Panther tattoos on his legs and all!

Never before, even at the great Middlesex Sevens at Twickenham, has one come across such a distinctive rugby audience as that in the Government Stadium in Hong Kong. It has become almost part of the tradition there that they greet the Southern Hemisphere hot shots, New Zealand and Australia, with an ocean of booing and their opponents with wild applause. Such support for the underdog, however, is all part of the good-natured atmosphere because, once the heavy artillery have shown their class in victory, they are treated to deafening ovations. Indeed, one suspects that the All Blacks and Wallabies would be a bit miffed if they did not receive flak at the start of their ties, safe in the knowledge that acknowledgement of their massive talents would follow at the end.

Naturally there was instant support for the Irish Wolfhounds and the Barbarians, worthy representatives from the British Isles, although it is time for the home countries to accede to the wishes of the organising committee and send out full national squads, just as the other 22 countries do, and thus put a final seal on the prestige of the Hong Kong event. The Wolfhounds, formed in 1956 by the former Lions captain, Dr Karl Mullen, had one of the most exciting runners in the tournament in Tony Underwood of Leicester, brother of England wing, Rory, and who scored four tries in three ties. And one of the loudest roars greeted the smash-and-grab try against Australia in the Cup quarter-final by 34-year-old Les Cusworth, who had played in the winning Barbarians seven at Hong Kong in 1981. Barbarians reached the semi-final with victories over Papua New Guinea, (26–0), Spain (24–4) and Canada (24–12), then seemed on the point of being put to the sword by the Wallabies who led 12–0 in next to no time. But with Llanelli and Welsh scrum-half, Jonathan Griffiths, in rare form, Barbarians staged a thrilling rally and, in retrospect, were wretchedly unfortunate that a bit of quick thinking by Scotland's Scott Hastings did not get its reward. He went over for Barbarians' first try, did not touch down at that point but got up to go nearer the posts to make the conversion easier. But the referee, Michael Hayden, who has had charge of some 70 ties in the Hong Kong Sevens, awarded the try where Hastings first crossed the line. Stuart Barnes was unable to convert. He did, however, convert a quite extraordinary try by John Jeffrey, his fourth of the tournament, that started out with faltering beginnings behind the Barbarians' goal line. But time ran out and the Wallabies won 12–10.

In 1988 Australia had beaten New Zealand in the final by 13–12. In 1989 they met in the final once again. The All Blacks had reached the final with 22 tries and 19 conversions for 126 points in four ties, the Australians with 21 tries, 17 conversions for 118. This time the All Blacks got their revenge by 22–10 through tries by a little human meteorite called Kevin Putt (2), the lightning quick John Schuster, and Canterbury flanker, Dallas Seymour. John

Zinzan Brooke, the victorious captain.

Gallagher's three conversions brought his tournament tally to four tries and eight conversions for 32 points. Australia had tries from Simon Poidevin and David Campese (his sixth), and Michael Lynagh's conversion brought his tournament total to five tries and 18 conversions for 56 points. Perhaps most impressive about the All Blacks' triumph was that their squad contained virtual unknowns outside their own country in Scott Pierce, Putt, Seymour, Eric Rush and Pat Lam, who fitted in as to the manner born and each of whom was capable of scoring from his own '22'. Nor did anything in the entire event match for sheer audacity and precision the perfectly placed surprise drop-out by, of all people, Zinzan Brooke, forward and captain, right into the path of a flying Seymour for the crucial try in the 12–10 semi-final win over Fiji who had not allowed the All Blacks into the match in creating an early 10–0 lead.

It was Fiji, however, who produced the winner of the Leslie Williams Trophy as the best and fairest player in the tournament, in Waisale Serevi, a 19-year-old cheeky chappie with impressive gifts of pace, change of direction and side-step, who scored five tries and ten conversions, and had the crowd roaring at his sinuous meanderings.

Where in the world except in Hong Kong would you find a referee from Thailand, who serves in the Royal Thai Air Force and possesses the unlikely name of Vengsakern Paerehitya, rubbing shoulders with such experienced officials as David Bishop of New Zealand and Gareth Simmonds of Wales? What a valuable learning process that must have been for Vengsakern.

From the very first tie in which the holders, Australia, ran in nine tries against Brunei, to the presentation of trophies by Gerry Forsgate, President of Hong Kong RFC, Willie Purves of Kelso, chairman of the Hong Kong Bank, and David Gledhill, chairman of Cathay Pacific, and the lap of honour by the victorious All Blacks, the Hong Kong Sevens showed the world of rugby in its most favoured guise as a magnificent sporting spectacle, reflecting immense credit upon Dermot Agnew, chairman of Hong Kong RFC, and his organising committee. No wonder players, officials and visiting referees all regard it as presenting a unique, rich experience, from the superb service provided by Cathay Pacific through Caroline Beecher in the UK and David Bell in Hong Kong, to the hospitality of the Hilton International, run like clockwork by their Fife-born manager, James Smith – all this against a background of sporting fellowship with friendly foes, old and new.

For one now described as a veteran television commentator, on his first visit, it proved a thoroughly rewarding experience, brilliantly organised, team and scoring information relayed to all the media representatives with timely precision and the vivid action on the pitch making commentary so pleasurable. Albeit there was a measure of relief among the English-speaking team of Ian Robertson of the BBC, Keith Quinn of New Zealand, Gordon Bray of Australia and myself that we were not called upon to pronounce at pace such names as Spain's Gerretxategui, Sri Lanka's Kethalawala, Ekanayake and Lakshantha, not to mention Taipei's two Chi-Mings, one Yen-Ching and one Chijen-Shuen and the three Kims and two Hongs in the South Korea squad! It was hard enough for us to sort out the three Raulini brothers, Viliami, Meli and Vesi, in the Fiji side! The expatriate community in Hong Kong were kindness itself, as were the flight crew of the Cathay Pacific Jumbo on the homeward journey. They allowed us the privilege of viewing from the cockpit the landing at Gatwick, a thrill in itself as a joyous and unforgettable experience in Hong Kong was brought with calm efficiency to a smooth and happy end.

WORLD CUP PRELIMINARIES
by CHRIS THAU

The 1991 World Cup has kicked off spectacularly in France in April 1989. The chief organiser, a pragmatic and cool Frenchman by the name of Daniel Coumeigt, branded the first qualifying round of the World Cup as a moderate success. The participants, Sweden, Denmark, Israel and Switzerland, and the International Rugby Board World Cup Director, Ray Williams, hailed the week-long tournament as a considerable success for the game and for the participating nations. The format of the round-robin tournament has vindicated a World Cup structure put forward in last year's annual and in *Rugby World and Post*. The games, though technically imperfect, have been hard fought, though from time to time the teams changed gear to produce some breathtaking moments of quality rugby. In addition, the infectious enthusiasm of the ninety odd players and ten or so organisers – a special mention for the immense efforts of Daniel Coumeigt and his two assistants, Philippe Briat and Catherine Dubois – conferred on the tournament in Tours the unique intensity of a World Cup pool. It was genuine World Cup rugby, though Israel with only eight clubs and about 400 players, and Switzerland with a playing population of about 1,000, are hardly powers to be reckoned with even by moderate international standards.

The poverty of the four Unions involved gives their Corinthian endeavour to take part, to be there and to play international rugby, a romantic image. Each Swiss player had contributed about £100 to make the tour possible, the Israelis were almost bankrupt, while the Swedes had squeezed every penny

Tounament Director Ray Williams (centre) watches the first skirmishes of the 1991 World Cup with local organiser Daniel Coumeigt on his left.

from their budget to raise the £12,000 needed to take part.

"We know that none of us has a chance of reaching the last 16. For all four nations this *is* the World Cup. It will do a lot of good to the game back home. For all of us, taking part is far more important that winning", so said Jean-Jaques Zander, one of the Swedish officials.

Zander, a French-born Swede, has been both the inspiration and the driving force behind the Tours tournament. The former US Tours hooker has had to convince reluctant international officials that his project was worth giving a try. "We have not received help from anyone. The International Rugby Board has supported our project, but we were told that there was no money in the kitty to give us. We have asked them to introduce us to some of the potential sponsors for the 1991 World Cup, but we were told that no sponsor has been approached yet. I tried to talk to the Federation Internationale de Rugby Amateur (FIRA), as all four countries are FIRA members, to convince them to undertake the project. I approached them with a plan to organise the tournament in France in one of the strong rugby regions: Burgundy, Ile de France, Côte d'Argent, or Languedoc-Roussillon, but to no avail. They did not even reply to our letters and telexes. It was quite amusing that at the recent FIRA Congress in Moscow, the French FIRA officials have listed the World Cup qualifier as one of the successes of FIRA. Eventually, in February 1989 I rang my old friend, Daniel Coumeigt, in Tours and asked for help. He said that we will try. Two days later he rang back : 'You are on', he said."

Daniel Coumeigt, an insurance broker, is the President of the Committee of the departement of Indré-et-Loire in the French Federation and vice-president of the successful second division club US Tours. Coumeigt managed the impossible and within two months from his conversation with his old pal Zander, he had the sponsors – two insurance giants Groupama and Société Générale – line up and the event was ready to start.

"It was hard work. My wife threatened to walk out on me at least 20 times. But in spite of everything we succeeded. But I have to say that without the help of about 30–40 volunteers from the nine small clubs involved in hosting the event we would never have succeeded. We did not want a scrappy operation. We wanted to treat players by top international standards. This was World Cup rugby, and the standard had to match the importance of the event", Coumeigt said.

Deservedly, Sweden won the competition. Captained by their giant number 8, Kari Tapper, now playing for Aberavon in Wales, the Swedes showed glimpses of class, which made them a tough proposition in their subsequent encounters with the Czechs, and the Dutch.

Sweden's giant captain Kari Tapper towers over his colleagues.

"Our victory reflects a major change of attitude of both our players and coaches. They take the game more seriously now. The old attitude, that rugby is just an opportunity for socialising, is slowly disappearing", said Swedish coach, Stefan Landgren.

The former Headingley coach, Bernard White, in charge of the Danish national team, is confident that such a competition can help to improve the standard among the lesser nations.

"The competition was magic and it will do a lot for the game in Denmark", he said. For the Israelis, on their first major tour abroad, this was the experience of a lifetime. "This tournament has put us on the map. For all of us this was our World Cup and will be the highlight of our playing careers. I will never forget the hospitality and the friendship with which we have been surrounded over here", said Israeli flanker Mark Notelovitz, one of the best players of the tournament.

Israeli flanker Mark Notelovitz.

The Swiss, oddly enough one of the oldest playing nations in the world, produced some moments of genuine magic when the brilliant outside-half, Eric Planes, formerly of Graulhet in France, joined them in the second half of their thriller against Sweden. "It was a huge success. What impressed me more than anything else was the way the teams improved during the tournament. Naturally playing three internationals in five days is quite demanding, but the 1991 World Cup is now truly launched and it has got a very good send off", concluded World Cup Executive Director, Ray Williams.

The qualifying saga will continue until the end of 1989 and on into 1990, with a four-team tournament involving Romania and Italy, both participants in the 1987 event, plus two qualifiers from an earlier Madrid tournament, the USA, Canada and Argentina series in North America, and the Asian/South Pacific tournament in which South Korea, Japan, Tonga and Western Samoa will battle for the two Asian slots.

THE SOVIET STUDENTS

The Shape of Things to Come
by CHRIS THAU

The Students' World Cup set in the magnificent surroundings of Bordeaux, the Basque Country, and Languedoc-Roussillon regions in the South West of France, was an unqualified success. The epic final between New Zealand and Argentina must have convinced even the doubting Thomases about the tremendous potential and quality of student rugby and the validity of the concept. The event has confirmed the supremacy of New Zealand rugby, winners of their second world crown in as many years. The tournament has unearthed players of considerable talent and ability who will no doubt leave their mark on the game in the near future. New Zealand number 8, Kevin Schuler, was described as a Wayne Shelford in the making, while the Argentine outside half, Diego Dominguez – invited to play for Steele-Bodger's XV against Cambridge University at the beginning of the last season – displayed touches reminiscent of his great predecessor Hugo Porta. Brian Gilchrist, Andy Sutton, Colin Laity, Mark Hancock, Tony Underwood, Andy Mullins and Victor Ubogu gave a good account of themselves, while Cameron Glasgow, Mike Hall and David Bryant showed glimpses of genuine class. The organisers, the French Student Federation, and Monsieur Michel Bonfils in particular, deserve a cheer for having created the event in the first place, and for their selfless and efficient efforts in its success. The tournament also announced the birth of a Soviet challenge in rugby. The Soviet Union, fourth in the tournament, enjoyed the unique distinction of beating the eventual world champions, New Zealand.

Previously the Soviets beat both England, after an ill-tempered match which showed some of the less savoury aspects of the Soviet approach to sport, and the Scots in a much more entertaining game which confirmed their seemingly inexhaustible resources of fitness and resilience. The Scots tried bravely to contain the immensely strong Soviet team, and to their credit managed to threaten the Soviet line on a number of occasions, but they were forced to acknowledge defeat, 19–11, at the hands of a stronger outfit. Following the World Cup clash, the Soviet students were invited back to Scotland for a short tour: a re-match against their Scottish counterparts and two other encounters against the Co-Optimists and a British Isles student selection.

Having sensed the growing interest in Soviet rugby, Kaiser Bautechnik, the Scottish Students' sponsors in the World Cup offered to finance a re-match between the Scots and the 'Bears', and the tour – the first ever by a Soviet representative to Britain – was on.

In the first match of the tour their comparatively tame performance and subsequent defeat against an under-strength Scottish Students side at Hughenden confirmed their lack of match practice. Captained by Scottish Students World Cup number 8, Alan Murray, and with Scotland 'B' centre Crawford McGuffie shining at outside-half, the Scots won a rewarding and well-deserved win by a try, two penalty goals and a drop goal to two goals to revenge their World Cup misfortunes.

Skipper Murray, a 22-year-old medical student at Manchester University, was naturally delighted: "It was a great team effort and I am genuinely happy that we won. We had not played together as a side before this match. We only met before the game, but what a great effort from the lads."

Understandably, the Soviets looked sombre after the game. Coach, Eduard Kobozev, described the performance of his team as inept and the worst ever by a Soviet side, while captain, Andrei Kirpa, seemed inconsolable. But a hard training session the following morning helped the tourists to recapture their habitual cheerful mood. National coaching director and Secretary of the Soviet Rugby Federation, Eduard Taturyan, on tour as an observer and adviser, summed up the feelings of the Soviet party: "Though disappointed,

The Soviets on their way to victory over the Scots in the Students' World Cup.

I am not too down-hearted. We made too many errors both individually and as a unit. But this is understandable. Our season does not start until mid-April and our players are quite rusty. However, I am quite confident that we can improve in the next game despite the formidable opposition. The Co-Optimists will be by far the strongest side we have played against. In a sense, the stronger the opposition, the better for our players. We have nothing to lose, but our inhibitions."

The performance of the Soviet Students against a star-studded Co-Optimists with seven full Scottish internationalists confirmed Taturyan's cautious optimism. Though forced to concede an early try, the Soviets bounced back with a vengeance and, with hooker Sergei Moltchanov – arguably the man of the tour – leading the surge from the front, they battered the Scottish pack into submission.

The Soviet backs, inspired by the powerful display of their forwards, ran riot with the nippy Siberian winger, Igor Kuperman, and classy Georgian fullback, Nougzar Dzagnidze, outstanding. Unable to establish a credible forward platform – which taking into account the formidable quality of the Scottish pack seemed quite surprising – the Co-Optimists had to rely instead on the boot of Melrose's Iain Ramsey.

The Soviet forwards displayed the ingredients, conspicuously absent against the Scottish students, that won them praise during the World Cup – graft, skill and an admirable appetite for combat. Besieged in their own territory, the Scots were genuinely relieved to hear the final whistle of Scottish international referee, Brian Anderson.

Though defeated, the Soviets were beaming after the game. Indeed there was a world of difference between their uninspired display at Hillhead and their sterling show at Meggetland. "This was much nearer our true potential", said coach, Taturyan.

The off-the-field activity of the tourists matched their busy playing schedule. Before the game against the Scottish Students they had been entertained by the Deputy Lord Mayor of Glasgow, while in Edinburgh they were hosted by the organisers of the first Science and Technology Festival.

The Soviet tourists met their Scottish student counterparts for an immensely enjoyable evening of traditional Scottish entertainment at Edinburgh University, when the entire audience joined the hosts for a session of Scottish folk dancing. A night at a discoteque in Kirkcaldy on Friday had set the entire party in the right mood for the following day's sevens in St Andrew's. Welcomed by SRU Midlands District representative, J.H.R.Wright, the Soviets enjoyed a lavishly laid lunch in the historic St Andrew's clubhouse. The Soviets managed to survive two rounds in the 57th sevens tournament, beating Carnoustie 6–4 and dispatching Montrose 22–0, before going down 10–6 to a slicker, and more competent Dunfermline, in the third round. The much improved performance of the Soviet forwards against the Co-Optimists the previous Thursday had given the Soviets good reasons for optimism. They hoped that the final game of the tour would bring about that elusive first win on Scottish soil.

The prospect of playing at Murrayfield, graciously offered to the Scottish Students' Union by the SRU, provided the visitors with an additional incentive to do well in their final outing of the week-long tour. Without two of their top backs, Korilihin and Hvedelidze, injured in the first game of the tour, the Soviets did very well to emerge victors 19–13 against a strong British Students XV, featuring emerging stars of the likes of David Evans of Wales, Adrian Davies and Rob Wainwright of Cambridge University, Shane Monro, Ford Swanson and Crawford McGuffie of Scotland 'B', and the resourceful Irish outside-half, Nick Barry, of the Garryowen club.

After the match, Kaiser's MD, Richard Nawrot, presented the Soviet captain, Andrei Kirpa, with a £1,000 cheque for the Armenian disaster fund and had the pleasure of presenting the winners' trophy to the Soviets at the post-match banquet held at the Caledonian Hotel in Edinburgh. The historic first ever tour to Britain by a representative team from the Soviet Union had ended on a high note, and the success of it, on and off the field, gave the RFU high hopes for an equally successful outcome for the senior Soviet tour scheduled for December 1989.

An enthusiastic Scottish welcome for Soviet captain Andrei Kirpa.

THE SOUTH AFRICAN CENTENARY
A Celebration or a Crisis?

The South African Rugby Board's Centenary celebrations in the autumn provided the most controversial talking point of the whole year as arguments raged about the rights and wrongs of sporting links and boycotts with a country hamstrung by its appalling policy of apartheid.

The dilemma facing the international rugby players from the Home Unions, France and Australia was immense as they received conflicting advice from a wide variety of sources. In the end a reasonably strong squad was assembled in Johannesburg around the 15th of August and it was further strengthened the following week when a group of top Welsh internationals arrived immediately after completing a weekend's training in preparation for their match against New Zealand in November. Ironically, much of the heated discussion emanated from New Zealand. Their Union was the only major International Board Union not to be involved in the Centenary Celebrations.

With the Commonwealth Games scheduled for Auckland in January it was deemed inappropriate by all concerned for there to be any approach to the All Blacks. Indeed there were loud clarion calls from New Zealand for the other nations to boycott the tour and ensure there would be no disruption to the Commonwealth Games. Apparently, the Auckland Games Committee very conveniently forgot or simply chose to ignore the fact that the last major tour of huge significance to South Africa, albeit an unofficial tour, was made by the New Zealand Cavaliers – the New Zealand All Blacks by any other name – in the summer of 1986.

There seemed a certain element of hypocrisy both in New Zealand and Britain in demanding England's expulsion from the Commonwealth Games when, if England were to be axed from the Auckland Games for allowing rugby links with South Africa in 1989, New Zealand should also have been expelled from its own Games because the last international tour to South Africa in 1986 was made up exclusively of very famous All Black players.

It has become quite clear in recent years that attitudes towards South Africa have hardened. Even though the game of rugby has become more multi-racial than ever before, the political system and regime of apartheid has made only marginal progress in the late 1980's. England made the most recent official tour in 1984 to South Africa, but it is extremely unlikely that any of the four Home Unions will tour officially to South Africa in the future until the political climate there changes quite substantially. It follows that the

Home Unions will also choose not to combine as the British Lions to tour South Africa.

This means in simple terms of fully fledged international competition there is no possibility at all of the Springboks touring to any of the major International Board countries in the near future and very little possibility of any individual country playing in South Africa. The only alternative for South Africa is to invite individual players from the top rugby nations to make up a composite World XV and that is what happened in August 1989.

The Unions in England, Scotland, Ireland, Wales, France and Australia were approached to pass on invitations to players to join a World XV to take part in a five match tour including two 'Tests'. The Unions certainly did not encourage any players to go but merely passed on the invitations and allowed each individual his democratic right to make up his own mind about whether he wanted to go and play in South Africa or not. The South African Rugby Board issued all the invitations after choosing the team they wanted and the Home Unions played a passive role in handing on the letters.

The Unions accept that world opinion will not tolerate major national tours to South Africa in the present political climate, but they believe individuals have the right to decide for themselves whether or not they wish to have sporting links with South Africa. Just as white South Africans like Gary Player are welcomed with open arms every year for the last 30 years at the British Open Golf Championship with not one single anti-apartheid demonstration, and white South Africans, similarly, are welcomed at Wimbledon every year, play very successfully in English county cricket every year, drive in the British Grand Prix and Gerrie Coetzee is allowed to box Frank Bruno in London, so individual sportsmen from Britain, it is argued, should be allowed to play in South Africa.

In the event, South Africa received a great many rebuffs before eventually cobbling together a decent party. They had hoped to include a large number of the highly successful British Lions side after their trip to Australia but a huge majority declined the invitation. Second and third choice players were then approached in England and Wales to make up the numbers when so many original selections decided against going. Several players in Wales stated openly they would not play in South Africa and then, dramatically, changed their minds and went. There were accusations that large sums of money had been offered but with no proof of any such temptations, no action was taken.

France provided the most top quality players but when the tour was badly floundering a fortnight before the first game in Durban on August 19th an SOS was sent to Australia. Six top Wallabies were invited including Nick

Farr-Jones, Michael Lynagh and David Campese but all declined. The invitations kept flooding in and at the last minute half-a-dozen Australians did accept at the same time as a few Welsh players changed their minds and also accepted. The tour was saved but only just.

With the formidable Irishman Willie John McBride as manager and long-serving Australian Bob Templeton as coach, the party prepared for the most demanding of tours. The first match was won, but the four remaining matches all resulted in narrow defeats. On the face of it, this seems to add up to an unsuccessful trip, but considering the multi-national mixture of the team and the ridiculously short time between assembling in Johannesburg and playing the two 'Tests' they staged remarkable recoveries to get within striking distance each time and they made South Africa work hard for their wins.

In the final analysis the actual results matter less than the fact that South Africa were able to have a tour by a World XV to help them celebrate their Centenary. At the same time and equally significant is the knowledge that they will not be able to rely on similar tours in the 1990's. They now know that no official tour by an individual country from the Home Unions or a British Lions tour is remotely possible until the political system in South Africa changes. Furthermore players are unlikely to rush to join another composite World XV in the future without a great deal of persuasion. Rugby in South Africa is at the crossroads - a professional circus there no longer seems light years away.

Still the best in the world. New Zealand winger John Kirwan proves too strong as Argentina are crushed in the Second Test , and (below right) Wayne Shelford finds the going a bit tougher against Australia in the Bledisloe Cup match, but once again the All Blacks were the winners.

THE LIGHTER SIDE

POINTS FOR PERFORMANCE

An Exhausting Survey
by MIKE BURTON, MBM Sports Management

Mike Burton, former England and Lions prop, graduated from being one of the stars of the after-dinner circuit to becoming one of the great entrepreneurs in the rugby world. He is also the author of a controversial autobiography and three perceptive books on the people of rugby and their particular lifestyles.

An acknowledged expert in female behaviour patterns, Mike Burton recently undertook a programme of research into the attitudes of rugby wives / girlfriends towards their men and the game they love.

A series of in-depth interviews has resulted and the manuscript is currently with the lawyers. A summary of some of the findings is all that can be revealed at this stage.

A STATISTICAL SUMMARY

Husbands who are regularly pissed as a result of rugby:
98%
(regular meaning more than once a week)

Husbands who are in their wife's view sexually satisfactory:
61%
(satisfactory in that she hasn't gone off yet but has complained after recent performances)

Husbands who are sexually satisfactory when they get round to it and not as active as they should be:
71%
(Active meaning more than once a month)

Marriages that have broken down as a direct result of rugby:
19%
(14% of the wives re-married a team mate of their first husband)

Marriages under severe strain because of the husband's rugby:
54%
(The percentage went up to 61% in marriages where the husband played cricket during the summer months)

Marriages that are happier because of the husband's involvement in rugby:
31%
(*Wives in these marriages are also members of women's rugby teams*)

Women who are glad they married a rugby player:
42%
(*58% don't know*)

Women who don't mind him playing but wish he would grow up:
65%

Women who discovered their husbands sexually unsatisfactory after the game and alcohol:
41%
(*59% were too pissed themselves to give an opinion*)

Husbands who refused to provide sex three days before a match:
3%

Husbands who became more sexually active in the closed season:
9%
(*the closed season being the week between the 7s and the Summer tour*)

Husbands prepared to help in the house on Sunday after the game:
14%
(*includes gardening, washing up and walking the dog*)

Husbands who bought more than six Sunday newspapers to see if they were mentioned:
82%

Wives who worry about injury when their man is playing rugby:
12%
(*14% of those asked said they wouldn't care if he never came home*)

Retired players and committee men who are more sexually active since they have become non-players:
89%
(*this figure was provided by the same cross-section of wives but did not necessarily refer to their own husbands*)

20 QUESTIONS
A Rugby Quiz

RUGBY HISTORY

1 Who were the opponents in the first ever Barbarians match, and in which year was it played?

2 Who was the founder of the Barbarian FC?

3 What particular distinction do the following rugby clubs have in common: St Paul's School; Harlequins; Guy's Hospital; Richmond; Blackheath; Civil Service; Wellington College?

4 Name the Englishman who never played against New Zealand for his country or the Lions, yet was a member of two teams which have defeated the All Blacks?

5 During the decade 1969–1979 Wales won 3 Grand Slams and six Triple Crowns. Who were the six players to captain Wales in one or more of the matches in those six seasons?

6 Two clubs, between them, provided the entire three-quarter line and half-back pairing during Scotland's first Grand Slam of 1925. Which were the clubs; who was the one 'outsider' (and also the captain) in the back division in that Grand Slam season?

7 Who was Ireland's one and only Grand Slam captain, and in which year?

8 Which Frenchman has been captain and coach of a Grand Chélem side?

9 Who was captain of the first World Cup-winning team?

10 In which year was *Rugby World* magazine (now *Rugby World and Post*) first published, and who was its first editor?

CLUBS AND PLAYERS

11 Which players have, or had, the following nick-names: Le petit général; Dusty; Budge; Cowboy; Mighty Mouse; Coochie?

12 Which clubs play at Anglesea Road; Goldenacre; Poynder Park; The Gnoll; Rodney Parade; Moss Lane; Imber Court; Kingsholm?

13 Who are the only two brothers to have represented the British Isles in the same Test match in the 20th Century?

14 Who scored the most points on the Lions Tour of Australia, 1989?

15 Which rugby players wrote the following books: 'Mud in Your Eye'; 'Dai for England'; 'Ripley's Book of Rugby Rubbish'; 'Everywhere for Wales'?

16 Which clubs are known as 'The Scarlets'; 'The Cherry and Whites';'The Quins'; 'The Wasps'; 'The Tigers'; 'The Greens'; 'The Black and Ambers'?

17 What have the following two international players in common: Enrique Rodriguez and Acura Niuqila?

18 Which clubs won the first-ever knock-out Cups in Wales (the Schweppes Cup), and England (the RFU Club Competition)?

19 Which player made the most consecutive international appearances in a career – and how many matches in the sequence?

20 Who captained the teams of the four Home Unions in the first World Cup?

(for the answers see page 129)

LOOKING BACK

25 YEARS AGO

From the pages of *Rugby World* during 1965 season

January 1965

Bert Goodwin, that estimable character from Coventry, has been telling people what it costs him to play rugby. A piece-worker in a factory, with a wife and young family, he loses 2 days' wages – up to £8 – every time he is picked for a trial or international match.

"It cost me more than £400 of the family savings to make the Lions tour of South Africa in 1962", he has said. Yet he no doubt thinks it was worth it.

Bert Goodwin of Coventry.

Right A try for Brian Price and Newport.

Cardiff and Maesteg are the latest clubs to have floodlights. Cardiff are delighted with theirs, a bargain buy at under £8,000. Equally important, Cardiff will be able to move them lock, stock and barrel when they move to the adjoining cricket ground and hand over the Arms Park to the W RU for development into a national ground.

Every country has its quota of players who ought to have been capped and were not, and who are remembered long after many of the lesser international performers have been forgotten. "International Class" means a different thing to different people. If many better players than Derek Brown of Melrose have played for Scotland, so, equally certain, have many worse.
Norman Mair

February 1965

"I have been criticised for not being aggressive enough, but when one player in a side is being over-aggressive it leaves only 14 men to play against opponents."
Brian Price (Newport and Wales)

A lot of fuss was made about the case of W. Mainwaring, the Aberavon forward, who was sent off the field by a London referee when playing for his club against London Irish.

What incensed some people, apparently, was not so much that Mainwaring was sent off, but that he was suspended automatically until his case came up before the WRU. This meant that he had to miss the first Welsh trial.

When his first case finally did come up he was found "not guilty" by the WRU....

It is wrong that a player should have been prevented from playing on even one Saturday if eventually he is going to be found innocent.

Royal High School ... have an outstanding prospect in their fly-half, C. M. Telfer.
Schools' Rugby Round-up

March 1965

"Four times this season I have come across cases of players being bitten by opponents – and in important matches! In two cases the victims have shown me their wounds personally ... the other two cases, that of Geoff Frankcom, the Cambridge University centre in the Wales v England match, and of Phil Judd, of Coventry, have already received publicity elsewhere".
Vivian Jenkins

Llanelli's Terry Price is the third post-war player to win his first Wales cap (against England) at 19. The others were Lewis Jones and Terry Davies. Both toured with the British Lions and collected most of the game's honours. Price, many feel, is destined to follow the same path. He is the fifth senior cap from the tiny Carmarthenshire village of Hendy, where he was born and still lives.

I don't subscribe to this view (*that the game's become*

more dirty). This is a game where you are bound to have a certain amount of give and take. I can remember my own playing days. I'd say the game's not as rough as it was then.
Tom Berry, chairman, England selectors

Hughie McLeod is the subject of many a Border anecdote. However, writing as a former hooker, my own favourite memory of McLeod is of his inquiring, with a deliciously expressive turn of phrase, as to whether or not I required him to disrupt the opposing hooker and loose-head prop .... "Shall I fork them, Norman?"
Norman Mair

The older you get the less attractive you find the really hard grind of training – but remember that with experience you learn to pace a match.
Bill Mulcahy, Bective Rangers, Bohemians and Ireland

Actress Elizabeth Taylor, with husband Richard Burton, was an 'extra' in the crowd at Cardiff Arms Park when Wales beat England. Before the game 'Liz', wearing a red Derby-style hat with a feather in it, disposed of a pint of beer in the true pre-match tradition of so many rugby watchers, and players! The Welsh forwards turned in a terrific performance in mud and driving rain to dominate the play ....
T. Price, the 19-year-old-boy, made a satisfactory debut.
Wales v England, 14–3, Cardiff

April 1965

The late O. L. Owen, doyen of rugby writers and for 43 years the rugby correspondent of *The Times*, made an immense contribution to the game ... The greatest outside he ever saw, he said, was W. J. (Billy) Wallace, the utility back of the 1905–06 All Blacks.

Bath have been having a disappointing season, their main problem being the lack of adequate reserves to bring into the top-class game.

Stan Purdy, formerly of Rugby and now with Fylde, ended a Coventry monopoly when he played for Warwickshire in the county semi-final against Surrey at Twickenham. This was his 50th appearance for the county – a feat only previously achieved by Coventry trio Phil Judd (60 consecutive

Left The young Colin Telfer.

games and still going strong), George Cole, on 55, and John Gardiner, first to the target, on 54. Purdy is finding Northern rugger a change from what he was used to in the Midlands. "There's much more running about to do", he says.

As a young journalist I lived with the Northampton players for six seasons. Once they removed my trousers in a Cardiff hotel and told the manager there was a sex maniac in the lounge! On another occasion they left me with a 60-mile hitch-hike over the Cotswolds from Cheltenham when they drove the coach off without me.
Barry Newcombe

Rugby tours for the most part are not what they were – which perhaps is a good thing. The days when boisterous lads barged into seaside hotels, smashed things up, kept people awake at night, paraded the streets in the early hours, threw deck-chairs into the sea and eggs at hotel proprietors, are on the wane ... a chap grows out of it, and the new generation finds little encouragement to carry on the tradition.
Rupert Cherry

Training started early last September when 25 boys (including Gareth Edwards) volunteered to return to school early in order to get themselves as fit as possible and acquaint themselves with the new laws. They were housed in tents and lived a spartan life.
Sydney Hill, master i/c rugby, Millfield School, (writing on the 'secret of Millfield's success')

May 1965
Clive Rowlands emerges as the man of the 1964–65 season at home. To have led his team, Wales, to a Triple Crown triumph is an achievement that no

one can take away from him, and he can now cock a snook at his previous detractors. His tactical kicking has not always been appreciated by those who like to see the ball passed quickly along the three-quarter line, in the classical manner, but for match-winning purposes it has proved its worth.
Vivian Jenkins

Perhaps even more amusing was the occasion when I was selected to play for the Barbarians versus Swansea, but had to withdraw shortly before the match started. This was unknown to the referee, who had apparently made up his mind to curb any off-side tendencies right from the start. From the first scrum he blew a long blast on his whistle, then said loudly "Off-side, Voyce!" He did not realise that I was miles away at the time and the player he actually penalised was my old friend A. F. (now Sir Arthur) Blakiston. Much to the discomfort of the embarrassed referee, players on both sides roared with laughter!
Tom Voyce

(R. J.) McLoughlin, by all accounts, encouraged and persuaded his men to eat and sleep, think and practise rugby in the 36-odd hours preceding an international in a bid to make them do the right thing automatically, and as if by instinct.
... (this) should not be outside the range and scope of any club side – if only they used their training sessions to maximum effect.
Norman Mair

June 1965
The correct pattern (*for short tours*) is gradually emerging thus : a) to go at the end of one's own season, not at the beginning; b) to play not more than 5 or 6 matches, with only one international match, right at the end and c) not to play the first

Right Tom Voyce, as President of the RFU, is introduced to the London Counties team before their match against Paris at Twickenham.

Clive Rowlands receives a *Rugby World* award from Vivian Jenkins.

'Dusty Hare', a
portrait by Rod
Jordan.

Paul Ackford
dominates the
line-out in
England's victory
over France at
Twickenham.

The Scots
surround Serge
Blanco at Parc des
Princes.

Line-out
anticipation as
Wales lose to
Ireland at the
National Stadium.

The Black Hawks
squad from
Malaysia discuss
tactics during the
Singapore Sevens.

A mudbath for
Bath and Bristol in
the Pilkington
Cup.

Israel and
Denmark contest
an early World
Cup qualifier at
Tours.

Soviet pyramid in
the Student World
Cup in Moscow.

match until a full week after arrival. Such a tour could be fitted comfortably into a month and players need not be away from their homes and jobs for longer.
Editorial

My husband plays rugby practically every Saturday in white shorts, which I have to wash. Here are a couple of hints on how to get them clean.

First, as a new Mum, I have found that even the grubbiest shorts come out beautifully white, without too much scrubbing, if they are soaked in 'Nappisan' – generally used for soaking nappies.

Second, to remove bad grass stains use a mild mixture of methylated spirit and warm water.

It's easy if you know how.
Reader's letter: Mrs C. M. Payne
Chiswick, London W4

I am a schoolboy and I think it is a disgrace that rugby-loving countries such as France should be refused a seat on the International Board.
Reader's letter: R. Sheehan,
Dublin 6

The main tactics for any team at any time must be to win, especially in international football … The end, I feel, justifies the means … (in the championship) I kicked frequently in support of my pack, as that was our main first-phase offensive weapon.
Clive Rowlands

The International Board has come under fire in France for not allowing the Australians to meet Romania after their 1966–67 trip to Britain … under an article "Splendid Isolation", *Midi Olympique* reported:"It must be made clear whether the world of rugby is to be as stupid as the world of politics and pretend that European rugby doesn't exist …"

"The form revealed by Australians Ken Catchpole and Phil Hawthorne in the trials for the matches in June against the Springboks has led many enthusiasts to claim that they are the finest pair of half backs in the world today."
Eddie Kann, Sydney

Ian Laughland receives the Russell-Cargill Memorial Cup on behalf of London Scottish after the Middlesex Sevens.

July 1965

It is one of the ironies of modern international rugby that Ian Laughland, whose game with London Scottish in seven-a-side and even in fifteen-a-side rugby rests primarily on his elusive running, is liable to be remembered by spectators as a utility player, excelling in cover defence – despite his miss and partial recovery in pursuit of Hancock – and as an ubiquitous opponent in broken play.
Norman Mair

Usually a third of the population in the valley will turn up and pay to watch the games. Throughout the day teams arrive by horse, lorry, boat, bus and on bare foot. Matches go on until dark, with never a pause, unless it is for the players of one game to lend their boots to those taking part in the next. So Saturday becomes a social event, which goes on with dancing to guitars until midnight. Then begins the long trek home.
Derek Robinson,Hon Sec Fiji RFU

The best pair of half-backs – as a pair – I have seen were Benny Jones and Dai Rees. I expect Davies and Kershaw were better, but they were before my time.
Alan Gibson, on the uncapped Welshmen
who played for St Lukes, Exeter and Devon

'Dull' rugby is confined almost entirely to international matches.
Reader's letter: John Wilson, N. Harrow

August 1965

Australia, suddenly right in the forefront of world rugby affairs, have set the International Board a new problem. The time has come, surely, when they must be allotted major overseas tours as an individual entity instead of being tagged on, as a kind of minor appendage, to the periodic tours of New Zealand.

Vivian Jenkins
(after Wallaby success v Springboks)

Right Richard Sharp on international duty.

There was a time when President White, of Cornell University, declared: "I will not permit 30 men to travel 400 miles merely to agitate a bag of wind" … It is not a "bag of wind" to say that the neat and modest appearance of the Combined Services team helped to offset the impresssion, current in North America, that young men in Britain comprise only Mods, Rockers and persons of indeterminate sex with Beatle hair-dos.

Colonel C. J. Reidy, Assistant Manager of Combined Services tour of Canada

Imagine, if you can, a mixture of Sevens, Soccer and Netball, and you have a mental picture of a most intriguing game which many London Rugby players take park in to keep themselves fit during the summer – Rugby Netball.

Rupert Cherry on events every Monday to Friday evening on Clapham Common

France's famous "rugby priest", the Abbe Henri Pistre, said after reading several reports of rough play: "What surprises me most is that certain leaders of the game seem only now to have discovered the cancer that is gnawing at the game in France … I dare not watch a game now for fear of weeping at the ferocity and open defiance of thirty young fellows … the players are not the only guilty ones".

September 1965

Richard Sharp's early retirement, at the age of 27, leaves a lamented gap. He has given tremendous pleasure in his all-too-brief career, even if his form had dropped off in the past year or two.

Vivian Jenkins
(Sharp was recalled to the England side v Australia in 1967!)

"It was a rugby player's dream. I found myself coming to the end of the match, and my only contribution had been a dropped pass. Any wing presented with the same opportunity in those closing seconds would have snapped up the try."
Andy Hancock, on his try v Scotland

Membership of the Rugby Football Union is now 2,359, schools affiliations numbering 791 … Planning application for the proposed South Stand at Twickenham has been withheld by the local authority …
The Union's surplus for last season, after taxation, was £48,081.

Andy Hancock in England's final trial in 1965.

October 1985

At the top, players must apply themselves more diligently concerning fitness, tactics and the laws. …Facilities have improved out of all recognition and clubhouses, changing quarters and catering facilities are very much part of the new set-up. Yet this side of the game must not be carried to the extreme, as it may militate against the game itself."
Bill Clement, Secretary, Welsh Rugby Union

Tonga were due to make their first overseas tour this year, to Queensland and New South Wales. Two hurricanes in four years, however, "knocked the economy for six" and it was impossible to raise the £4,500 for the trip.

There is a newly-formed Papua and New Guinea Rugby Union.

Six international defeats in a row is by Springbok standards a bit much. South Africa's tale of woe includes defeats by France, Ireland, Scotland, Australia (twice) and New Zealand…. In a radio broadcast Dr Craven came straight to the point. South African players, he felt, were "getting soft".

"I was amazed how drastic modern training methods can be. There were 80 of them going hard for an hour-and-a-half without a rest".
Wasps secretary, Neville Compton, commenting on Freddie Hawkins' club training sessions!

November 1985

Should the 'mark' be abolished? Some people think it should, on the grounds that a free kick seems too great a reward for merely catching a ball cleanly.

At about 7 o'clock I noticed that all the other girls had gone, and my worthy escort was looking meaningfully at his watch. The penny didn't drop and I sat cheerfully on, until a group of gentlemen in the corner began to sing some songs the like of which I have never heard before. Something about a girl called Dinah and a Mayor of Bayswater who, apparently, had a daughter. I beat a hasty retreat.
Margaret Jerome

Monmouth School have a notable player in their captain, A.M. Jorden, who is in his fourth season at fullback.

December 1965

The International Board has another problem on its hands. It must decide, sooner or later, how far commerical sponsorship is to be allowed in the game.
Editorial

Heard in the Swansea clubhouse after the visitors, Llanelli, had kicked their way to a shock win "If a rugby ball was meant to be carried, the Almighty would have put a handle on it".

In recent years Irish officials have built up a high reputation for intelligent application of the laws and for their fitness and ability to keep up with the fastest games. Han Lambert, Bobby Mitchell, Ray Williams and Kevin Kelleher have been the most sought-after referees over the last 20 years, their only rival being Welshman, Gwynne Walters.
Paul MacSweeney

After long years in the wilderness, the Club is near the top again.
Doddy Hay on Blackheath

Given a reasonable pack, the scrum-half is a match-winner – and he'll never get a cold on a January afternoon!
John E. Williams, Sale and England

Gwynne Walters consults the Cambridge touch judge during the 1964 Varsity Match.

DUSTY HARE

by CHRIS GODDARD

William Henry Hare came to terms with life without hair some time ago. Quite how Leicester will find life without Hare is another matter.

The greatest place kicker the game has ever known retired after a sentimental, but ultimately unrewarding, Pilkington Cup final against Bath last season, and Leicester acknowledge that a straight transplant would no more work for them than it would for Dusty.

"It would be wrong to try and find a Dusty clone," smiled Leicester secretary John Allen. "And anyway it would be nigh on impossible."

Even so, the Tigers' philosophy is that no one, but no one, is indispensable. After all, didn't they successfully replace the likes of Wheeler, Cowling, Adey, Woodward, Duggan and Barnwell?

Sure they did, and while they were all superb, influential players none of them could guarantee Leciester what Hare could – 10 points a match.

It was Hare's astonishing consistency which, according to his old mate Les Cusworth, was one of the secrets behind Leicester's success with their exciting, high risk brand of 15-man rugby.

"Because we knew that Dusty would always pop over at least 10 points it took the pressure off and allowed us to relax and express ourselves" he says.

So good was Hare at his job that it was impossible not to become rather blasé about his feats. I've forgotten how many times I've started my 'runner' for the Saturday sports paper with the words 'Hare gave Tigers the lead with a penalty', or finished it 'Hare clinched victory with a penalty (drop goal)'.

What Hare achieved in a career spanning two decades is well documented, but it's so mind bending that it's worth recalling. Consider, if you will, that the old world points record was 3,651 held by Sam Doble, who obliterated the scoring feats of marvellous kickers like George Cole and Peter Butler. Hare almost doubled that, and in all but one of his 13 years at Leicester, his début season, averaged more than 10 points a game. It tells a lot about the man's character that in his final season at an age – 36 – when most players find it easier to write about the game than play it, he not only broke his own club points record by amassing 434, but posted his best average of 13.5.

Records tumbled to Hare throughout his career, some he's not proud of, like managing to get himself dropped by England five times. It was about to become six in 1985 when Hare announced he'd had enough of the international treadmill, by which time he had collected a record 25 caps at fullback and scored a record 240 points.

And it's three of those he will perhaps be best remembered for, the injury time touchline penalty in 1980 which gave England a 9–8 victory over Wales and set them up for the Grand Slam. While the English fans were knee deep in chewed finger nails, Hare, who was so laid back he made David Gower look like Magnus Pike, stroked over a pressure kick to end all pressure kicks as if he was shelling peas.

"I could never understand why people got so nervous for me," he once said. "I never was, but then kicking was my job, and one I happened to be good at."

We might never have found out just how good, though, had Hare realised his ambition of becoming a professional cricketer with Nottinghamshire.

After a couple of years on the Trent Bridge groundstaff he decided he wasn't good enough, although it's probably fairer to say that his low concentration threshold was not as suited to cricket as rugby where at times he gave the impression of an Englishman on holiday. A hankie round his head and a deck-chair behind the posts were all that was missing.

Those endearing qualities, however frustrating they might have been to his team mates, were what made Hare such a special and watchable player.

The player who killed off the All Blacks for the Midlands at Leicester in 1983 with a 55-yard penalty and the best drop goal I ever saw, all of 65 yards, was quite capable of the most horrendous howler, usually the result of a Nureyev type pirouette and 'n' number of sidesteps on his own goal-line prior to being buried by the entire opposition pack.

"An errant genius," says his former coach and mentor, Chalkie White.

"Never predictable. But, you know, he was a considerably more skilful player than people gave him credit for. He had an insight into the game that could be measured against the best in the world.

"And he had an innate ability, not just kicking ability, that compared favourably with some of the great world class players."

White has known Hare ever since his grammar school days in Newark and, as coach, introduced him to first-class rugby with Notts, Lincs and Derby in 1970.

White was accused of poaching when Hare made the short trip down the A46 to join Leicester from Nottingham which, to anyone who knows Hare, is nonsense. He has always been his own man and, as he says, he moved simply "for a higher class of rugby" and to further his England chances.

He achieved both during a highly successful 13-year association with "the best club in England", during which time he became something of an institution, and a much loved one to boot.

Loved not just because of his extraordinary feats on the field but also his modesty and humour off it.

Head down as Dusty
Hare makes contact
fot the vital kick at
Twickenham in 1980,
and (inset)
congratulations from
Bill Beaumont and
Welsh prop Graham
Price.

More than anything Hare liked to enjoy himself to the full, not least after a game, although it sometimes proved rather painful. A couple of years ago after a night out in Swansea he collapsed on a settee on the first floor of a hotel only to find himself being propelled down the stairs a few moments later by two forwards. The porters who came out of the woodwork couldn't believe who it was when they eventually pulled the settee off a crumpled Hare.

Training wasn't his favourite pastime, and there must have been times when his team mates thought they would have to start a match with 14 men. He once strolled into the dressing-room 10 minutes before kick-off and White said: "You just couldn't tell him off. He has the bluest of blue eyes, so full of innocence."

When the folk of Hare's home village of South Clifton planted a tree in his honour, White and a few friends suggested it would be a good place to "stop for a pee" on the way home from the pub, which Hare neatly adapted by dedicating the monument to the local dogs who, he said, "never missed a chance to pay their respects."

Hare lasted so long simply because of his great love of the game. Indeed after casting off the yoke of what passed for an England jersey at the time he played better than at any time in his career, not least near the end when his line-kicking was quite extraordinary.

A final farewell at Twickenham after the Pilkington Cup final.

Hare wants to stay involved in the game and White reckons he would make a great Midlands selector, an apprenticeship that "ought to lead to the England panel."

White's love and respect for Hare is obvious. "I'd go to war with him," he says unashamedly.

"He leaves the game enhanced by his contribution. He had given more to it than he has taken from it, and if you can say that what else is there to say."

A Team from the Eighties

THE BACKS
selected by PHIL BENNETT

To be a successful selector – or a selector of any kind, for that matter – you need a very thick skin. That was one of the thoughts that crossed my mind when I was asked to pick my back division for the 1980s and, worse still, give the reasons for my choices. It is no easy job as I know from having been asked to stick my neck out so often before when I have picked Welsh teams, Lions teams and a lot of other sides, which fortunately have never taken the field to put my expertise to the test.

Anyway, here goes again! Fullback? With JPR Williams really a Seventies man I eventually narrowed my choice down to three players. Paul Thorburn is a great kicker and has won matches for Wales with his kicking, whilst Dusty Hare has done the same for England and was often underestimated in other aspects of his game; on his only Lions tour he was not properly used and was not able to do himself justice, but year in and year out his kicking was a model of consistency, and he did score a few tries into the bargain.

Nevertheless, my vote for the no 15 jersey would be Scotland's Gavin Hastings, who is not only a fine kicker, but also a powerful runner (quick for a man of his immense physique) and tackles well. Apart from John Gallagher, who as a New Zealander is not eligible for this selection, he is the best fullback in the world and must be my top choice.

On the right wing there were several good candidates starting with Ieuan Evans, for whom the Lions tour was absolutely vital as he has had so many set-backs to place against his good moments that he needed a good tour to establish his credentials permanently as a great wing. Another fine wing and great opportunist is Trevor Ringland, who was recently forced out of the game by injury; he was another who had an unlucky tour with the Lions in New Zealand in 1983 (like Dusty Hare), but for Ireland he was a fine player and was a vital part of the Irish Championship winning sides of 1982, 1983 and 1985.

My choice for the right wing, however, is an England player – John Carleton. He was not fast but he was a good taker of chances and had a fine football brain; in fact he seemed to be able to sniff out the line at the right time and the Scots will not forget his hat-trick of tries at Murrayfield in 1980 when England last won the Grand Slam.

At centre I always like one big man and one smaller, perhaps nippier one who can combine with him; they can in effect feed off each other. Candidates for the big position included David Irwin, who made quite a come-back last season even though he missed out on the Lions tour, and Alan Tait, who went to rugby league before he gave himself a real chance to make a proper mark on the union game. Even so, what we saw of him was most impressive and he was a star for Scotland in the 1987 World Cup.

But my big man would be Paul Dodge, who was not only strong and a difficult man to stop but had a superb kick in his left boot, which he often used to excellent effect. For Leicester he has always impressed in the way he has combined so efficiently with Les Cusworth. As a big, strong fellow he was always a good man to have around in wet conditions.

For the other centre spot I had a very tough choice between David Richards, who was really an outside-half but did well for Wales whenever he was called on to play at centre, where he used his eye for an opening and clever running to great effect. Another good candidate is Brendan Mullin, whose trip to Australia with the Lions was inconclusive in advancing his cause. He has been playing in a struggling Irish team, but back in 1984 when he first came on the international scene he looked as if he would carry everything before him – and he could still do it.

However, I remember what a small and elusive centre did to Wales at Cardiff in 1982, when the Scots thrashed Wales (34–18). That afternoon Jim Renwick gave us a terrible run-around and on other occasions I saw the way his clever running gave opposing sides nightmares. He was a silky runner with a superb dummy and, although the 1980 Lions tour in South Africa did not show him up in the best light, it had the same effect on several other good players, so that can be ignored.

On the left wing I can see only one player I want in my side, although there have been a number of good candidates. Mike Slemen was such a good footballer that he could have played in any back position – especially fly-half. As a wing he was one of those people who went looking both for the ball and the open spaces and, when he did have the ball, he was hard to nail because of his superb change of pace. He struggled at times in England teams which lacked confidence; and he was unlucky with his two Lions trips when the team struggled in New Zealand in 1983 and then he had to return early from the 1980 South African tour because his wife was pregnant. But he was nevertheless a Grand Slam winner with England in 1980.

Outside-half is the hardest of all positions to select because there have been several outstanding players in that area. There was Ollie Campbell, who was a great place-kicker and brave tackler; Gareth Davies, whose 1980 Lions trip was ruined by injury; Jonathan Davies , who was a superb all-round player but had not quite reached his best when he went to rugby league; and John Rutherford, an outstanding player for Scotland, particularly in partnership with Roy Laidlaw.

Jonathan Davies was great with the ball in his hands and had almost everything; if he had stayed with us for another year he might have taken the vote. But he did not and John Rutherford's 47 appearances for Scotland, in which he showed himself to be the complete player with his tactical kicking, dropped goals and superb dummies (just to mention a few of his many good points), won him my vote ahead of the others. He was another who was a good player on a Lions tour but was never given a fair crack of the whip in terms of Test chances.

So that leaves the scrum-half and there have been some excellent exponents of this art in Roy Laidlaw, so effective with John Rutherford; Nigel Melville, so unlucky with injuries; Robert Jones, who is a fine player and might win the vote one day – all magnificent players.

But the best of the decade for me was Terry Holmes, who had it all and, most of all, he had bravery. He may not have been as great as Gareth Edwards – who was? – but he was a 'no surrender man', who did everything well and was especially dangerous a few metres from the line, where he was lethal. Injuries played him too many bad deals, but that cannot stop him from taking the vote.

So there you have the names: Gavin Hastings, John Carleton, Paul Dodge, Jim Renwick, Mike Slemen, John Rutherford and Terry Holmes. Only write to me, please, if you agree!

How does this selection, or any rival assessment, compare with the backs of the Seventies? Well, the Seventies did turn out many world-class players such as Gareth Edwards, Barry John, JPR Williams, Gerald Davies and David Duckham. But the Eighties players may well have been more adventurous, fitter, stronger and faster and not that far behind their more famous predecessors. Comparisons may be odious, but they can also be fascinating. And how many of you can remember better games in the past than the matches at Cardiff in 1988 between Wales and Scotland or the recent Scotland–Ireland match at Murrayfield? It was great stuff.

THE FORWARDS
selected by BILL BEAUMONT

Whereas in the previous decade there were three Lions tours, of which two series were won and some great forwards took part such as Mervyn Davies, Fran Cotton, Gordon Brown, Willie-John McBride and so many others (you name them and you'll take a long time doing it), the Eighties had seen only two unsuccessful Lions tours before the eventual victory in Australia this summer. So there have been limited opportunities to assess form at the top. This makes selection difficult although there have, of course, been plenty of good forwards and I think you will find that my final choice would produce a superb pack.

At loose head it is a pity that Fran Cotton – really a man of the Seventies – cannot be considered, but some fine props have been on Lions tours such as Clive Williams and Staff Jones, although neither of them in my view approaches the sheer mobility and athleticism of David Sole, who has also improved his scrummaging immeasurably. He is already a very good player and could end up being a great one. He wins my vote.

Amongst several good hookers, including Colin Deans, Cieran Fitzgerald, Brian Moore and Alan Phillips, one man stands out – Peter Wheeler. He had everything that makes a man great in that position; he was a good striker for the ball, fine scrummager, good person to throw in to line-outs and was mobile around the field. I am not alone in thinking that he should have led the 1983 Lions and he is my choice.

There have been numerous fine tight heads also, but great ones are in short supply. Graham Price is one who could be considered, but he too probably belongs to the Seventies. Have we enough evidence yet to select David Young? Has Iain Milne, for all his fine work for Scotland, really been consistent enough and free enough from injury to merit selection? One tight head I know well, having played alongside him a few times for England, was Phil Blakeway. For pure scrummaging power as the cornerstone of the pack there was no one better, so he is my man for the no3 jersey.

With the great locks of the Seventies all unavailable for this pack the choice of a second row was as hard a task as any. There are some useful men like Donal Lenihan for the front jumping position and Paul Ackford has come on well over the last two seasons. Wade Dooley has also been a consistent line-out jumper at no 4 for England and I also rated Steve Bainbridge as a fine performer. But my two men would be Maurice Colclough as the front jumper, because he was also a marvellously solid scrummager, with Robert Norster as the middle jumper as he has had more experience and success at the very top

A team for the
Eighties:

15. Gavin Hastings

14. John Carleton
13 Jim Renwick
12. Paul Dodge
11. Mike Slemen
10. John Rutherford
 9. Terry Holmes

 1. David Sole
 2. Peter Wheeler
 3. Phil Blakeway
 4. Maurice Colclough
 5. Robert Norster
 6. Jeff Squire
 7. Peter
    Winterbottom
 8. Dean Richards

15

11

14

13

12

10

9

1

2

3

4

5

6

8

7

level than any of his challengers. At his peak he always seemed capable of getting the better of Wade Dooley and that must mean that he should be given preference.

The back row choices have been more numerous, but at openside flanker I come down firmly in favour of one player. There have been a number of recent successes in the position, notably Finlay Calder, the exciting Andy Robinson and Ireland's Nigel Carr, whose career was so sadly curtailed by that bomb injury. But in a poor Lions team in New Zealand in 1983 Peter Winterbottom was outstanding and on reflection I am amazed that he was not in the picture as far as England selection was concerned last season. I am sorry too that the Lions selectors did not take him to Australia, but he is my openside man for the Eighties.

Covering the blindside again has been no easy task because there have been some good candidates such as John Jeffrey, Phillip Matthews, Mike Teague and Jim Calder, but again I pick a man whose play I knew very well and respected. Jeff Squire could play at flanker or number 8, but as a blindside flanker his height made him more than useful at the tail of the line-out and he was both athletic and mobile in everything he did. He is my choice.

Number 8 provided a good number of excellent candidates such as John O'Driscoll, Iain Paxton (who did so well in a beaten Lions pack in New Zealand in 1983), Eddie Butler (an underrated player) and now Derek White, but my selected favourite is Dean Richards, who is one of the best I have ever seen and is particularly strong in defence. In fact, he is one of the very few out-and-out number 8s now playing and if there is any criticism I have to make of him it is that he might be rather stronger in defence than in attack, although I do appreciate that he has scored his fair share of tries for England.

So there it is. My eight would be David Sole, Peter Wheeler, Phil Blakeway, Maurice Colclough, Robert Norster, Peter Winterbottom, Jeff Squire and Dean Richards. And how about Peter Wheeler as captain of the whole of the Eighties team?

PREVIEW OF THE SEASON
1989–90

THE HOME CHAMPIONSHIP
by BILL McLAREN

Those of us privileged to see 'live' the Scotland v Ireland game at Murrayfield on March 4 will cherish the hope that the 1990 Five Nations Championship will be more liberally imbued than its predecessor with the same spirit of flowing adventurism that so marked that wonderful match.

The 1989 Championship did have its other moments. France's remarkable recovery from impending doom at Lansdowne Road revealed a quality of football of which only the French, totally on song, seem capable. That Scotland v Ireland classic brought eight splendid tries of contrasting and enthralling creation. England raised a huge well of emotional patriotism by subjecting France at Twickenham to their only championship defeat. Even in the squelch and slaister of a rain-soaked Cardiff Wales emerged from, for them, an unaccustomed long, dark tunnel with a hard-won, rivetting, if not very spectacular, triumph over England.

It was a heartening aspect of the 1989 Championship, too, that of the 33 tries scored (two more than in the previous season), 24 were by backs with the French backs, not surprisingly, holding pride of place, Serge Blanco scoring four, Patrice Lagisquet three, Pierre Berbizier two and Jean-Baptiste Lafond one. Try scoring in the Championship gave some pointer to the way teams played and perhaps also to some of their strengths and weaknesses. Scotland, for instance, did try to move the ball around and were second top try-scorers to France. Ireland's defence frailties could be measured by their concession of 12 tries in their four games and England proved the most parsimonious in having their line crossed only twice. Tries scored and conceded were as follows, with the corresponding figures for the previous season in brackets: France 11–3(8–3); Scotland 9–7(6–7); England 4–2(6–3); Wales 3–9(7–4); Ireland 6–12(4–14). Whereas the French backs scored 10 of their 11 tries, Scotland had the wider distribution, five by backs, four by forwards. Ireland's backs scored five, their forwards one, England had two by each section and Wales two by Mike Hall and one by Mark Jones.

On the basis of what they achieved, or failed to achieve, in the 1989 Championship, resolutions by each country for the 1990 campaign might be on the following lines:

France – to seek in every match the astonishing continuity of support and pass transferrance that led to perhaps the try of the championship as Serge Blanco strolled in under the bar unopposed against Ireland. That sequence of passes, which began as Frank Mesnel retrieved a charged-down Blanco clearance,

Lagisquet (above left), Lafond (above) and Blanco (left) score three tries for France against Ireland, Wales and Scotland.

Below Ivan Tukalo scores one of his three tries against Ireland.

gave a perfect illustration of how backs and forwards can intermingle in the true concept of total rugby, for the passes were delivered in the following order: stand-off, prop, prop, scrum-half, centre, fullback, right wing, fullback, number 8, prop, right wing, scrum-half, stand-off, scrum-half, centre, fullback.

Scotland – to achieve more of that kind of French interplay by which, for example, they created Ivan Tukalo's superb first of three tries against Ireland.

England – to hoist their tries tally to beyond the miserly four of 1989 and to maintain their immense forward power but not at the same expense of expansive play spread among their quick backs.

Ireland – to work harder on keeping fingers in the dyke so as not to leak so many tries, and to aim for more productive drive play by their pack.

Wales – to pray for no more defections to rugby league and to build on the confidence created by their spirited and tactically sound display against England.

Having won or shared the last four Championships France, the holders, remain the gauge by which the other four countries will measure their advance and status. After France's comprehensive defeat of Scotland in Parc des Princes on March 31 (Scotland last won in the Parc in 1920) Finlay Calder, Scotland's captain, in praise of France's performance that day, claimed that for several seasons "France have been the best side in the Championship" and on that afternoon would have beaten any side in the world, perhaps even the All Blacks. The 1990 Championship, however, could bring something of a new look French side. On the recent tour of New Zealand Jacques Fouroux continued to experiment. Mesnel, their championship stand-off, was played as wing then, in the First Test, as inside centre in preference to Marc Andrieu, to a new stand-off cap, Philippe Rouge-Thomas, a stocky, rumbustious type. There also was a new hooker in Dominique Bouet, while Thierry Dévergie was playing in only his second major international. The Championship may have also seen the last of such veteran forwards as Jean-Pierre Garuet (36), Jean Condom (29) and Dominique Erbani (33). French resources are so deep, however, that those who have wide experience of the French game reckon they could field three fifteens who could hold their own in the Championship although, significantly, in recent seasons France have not been notably successful at 'B' international level. The coming Championship may be just the time to topple them from their perch.

The Championship could also be given a handsome fillip if England were to rediscover that adventurous approach by which they overcame the Wallabies at Twickenham in November 1988. England came within a whisker of winning the title for the first time since Bill Beaumont led them to their 1980 Grand Slam, but their pattern was somewhat restricted with the ball seldom spun in the thrilling manner of that Australian game. England should still have a splendid ball-winning pack and the same high quality of mauling and broken play support work among the forwards.

Of course in their first championship game, the 12–12 draw against Scotland at Twickenham, England's midfield were subjected to a series of shuddering tackles and they subsequently resorted to a punt-and-pack format so that three of their four tries stemmed from close-quarter driving operations, formidable indeed as they were, and only one, that by Will Carling against France, from spreading the ball to midfield. England were unfortunate in that their matches against Ireland and Wales were contested in difficult conditions hardly conducive to a strategy carrying a higher risk factor. There could be keen rivalry for England's fullback role in light of Simon Hodgkinson's pinpoint place-kicking against the Romanians in Bucharest on May 13 – nine goals out of ten shots for 19 points on his cap début in victory by 58–3. England too must derive considerable benefit from their successful 'B' tour to Spain under the captaincy of David Pegler of Wasps. Yet the keenest desire of England's supporters will be to see more running opportunities for their exciting and very quick wings, in which regard the experience gained by Jeremy Guscott, Chris Oti and Rory Underwood with the Lions in Australia, not to mention the other nine Englishmen in the party, should contribute

The English contribution to the Lions team for the Third Test.

Scotland's exciting new halfback combination, Gary Armstrong (left) and Craig Chalmers.

Right Nick Barry, a promising member of the Irish squad.

towards England being an even mightier force in 1990.

The Lions tour is one factor that raises Scottish hopes of a successful 1990 campaign. When Scotland won the Grand Slam in 1984 for the first time since their only previous success in 1925, the broad nucleus of that side was formed by the eight players who had toured with the Lions during the previous summer. Those Scottish Lions gained in confidence on that tour. This time Scotland gave nine men to the Lions including the captain, Finlay Calder, and their two young halfbacks, Craig Chalmers and Gary Armstrong. That experience should enhance their contribution to the Championship.

Of course that 28–24 defeat by Japan in the last match of their tour there in May was a shattering blow to the Scots, although it has to be said that seven penalty chances were missed and on several occasions Scots were stopped just short of the Japanese line. Scotland, however, should have their full complement available for early season cap internationals at Murrayfield against Fiji and Romania, and they should be in good heart for the Championship in which they will start a fortnight after the others with an away match with Ireland on February 3. Another eight tries extravaganza assuredly would launch their 1990 Championship on the right note.

One exciting development towards Irish prospects is the acquisition of the Australian Test player, Brian Smith, who was included in their party to tour North America in August and September. Smith was capped by Australia initially as scrum-half but made a special impact as director of operations from stand-off when Oxford won the Varsity match in December. How Ireland will use him could be one of the most intriguing aspects of selection having regard to the wide experience of Paul Dean (32 caps), who was desperately unlucky to be injured in the Lions' first match in Australia and brought home for knee surgery, and also the challenge posed by Nick Barry of Garryowen who played so well when Ireland toured France in May 1988 and who looked a neat, quick, tidy

little player for the British students against the Soviet students at Murrayfield in April. Ireland must seek a higher ball-winning return, especially from breakdown points, if they are to repeat the positive attacking style that brought three very good tries by their backs against Scotland.

Wales could be on the mend. Lions coach Ian McGeechan has pointed to their second half display against Scotland at Murrayfield last season as hinting at high potential and, if they can reach the best balance in their loose forward trio and find a settled blend at halfback, they could make quite an impact. Their home games this season will be against France and Scotland. Their June tour to Canada enabled them the extend the dossiers on a number of young aspirants among whom the Llanelli stand-off, Colin Stephens, could make the breakthrough to the Five Nations and might become another in that distinguished line of gifted craftsmen from the Welsh fly-half factory.

Ireland and Wales also face the sternest preparation for the Championship for the All Blacks tour of some 13 games includes internationals against Ireland at Lansdowne Road on November 4 and against Wales at Cardiff Arms Park on November 18.

If Wales can get their act together it will make for a very open Championship with France and England front runners but facing a forceful challenge from the Celtic clans.

Colin Stephens of Llanelli.

Of much more importance than who wins the title, however, is that the Championship should be the mirror of all that is good in the rugby game so that the huge numbers keen to see the games will continue to be drawn there by the attraction of the fare provided, as much as for nationalistic motives. There is enough talent in the four countries to produce a title campaign marked by spectacular and exciting action. Indeed if each of the five countries reaches out in positive fashion for genuine total rugby so that each game has the flavour of that Scotland v Ireland classic last March, the 1990 Championship assuredly will be one to linger long in the memory.

KEY PLAYERS

ENGLAND

ROB ANDREW

ANDY ROBINSON

Against France last season Rob Andrew became England's most capped fly-half when he overtook the record of W.J.A. Davies, who won his caps both before and after the 1st World War. Andrew won his first against Romania in 1985 and his 26th when he captained England for the first time in their record-breaking win over Romania in Bucharest in May 1989. As befits a man who won a Cambridge Blue at cricket as well as rugby, he has an excellent pair of hands and is a natural ball-player. He kicks well with either foot and is one of the most aggressive tacklers to play international rugby at fly-half in recent seasons. In defensive tackling and covering duties he is one of those rare half-backs who covers as an extra flanker. Not initially a master tactician, he has learned by experience and had outstanding matches against Australia last November and against Romania this year. These performances were the highlight of England's most successful season since 1980, and, with Andrew running the backs and the tactics, he must take much of the credit Firmly established in the England side as they build up to the next World Cup, he will be the key figure during the next two years. He gained further valuable experience when he flew out as a replacement and played with great success with the Lions in Australia this summer. A prolific goal-kicker he has scored 137 points for England, including nine drop goals which is an English record, and 28 penalties.

Andy Robinson began his senior rugby playing for Loughborough, the English Students and the UAU. He joined Bath in 1986 and two years later won England 'B' caps against Italy and Spain. He became a member of the full England squad last year and helped Bath to win the Pilkington Cup and the Courage League, as well as being a regular member of the South West divisional side. Bath have just about the best pack in English rugby which is a great help to Robinson as he is surrounded by other top-class players who have helped him to develop his talents so quickly. Bath dominated the domestic season with their outstanding pack , but even in such august company Robinson stood out as the star forward. He went on tour with England to Australia in 1988, and played in all England's internationals since then. He toured Australia with the Lions in 1989, gaining more valuable experience, and will remain a crucial member of the England pack this season. He has remarkable speed across the pitch, seemingly unlimited stamina, is particularly good at winning the ball on the ground and has a natural insight into the game. He lacks height at the back of the line-out, but England have plenty of big jumpers, leaving Robinson free to concentrate on what he does best – be a destructive flanker in defence and a constructive one in attack. He has become the nearest the Northern Hemisphere can boast to the All Black phenomenon, Michael Jones.

FRANCE

SERGE BLANCO

PIERRE BERBIZIER

In a country which has produced many outstanding backs during the past 20 years none has been more influential than Serge Blanco, who developed very quickly into one of rugby's truly great players and who has maintained his exalted reputation for the best part of a decade. He won his first full cap against South Africa in 1980 and has played a world record number of 70 times for his country, overtaking the previous record of 69 held by Mike Gibson of Ireland. His great assets are his tactical ability and almost unlimited natural skill which have enabled him to make and to score a string of tries which lesser mortals would not even consider possible. He has blistering speed and accelleration as befits someone who has won 12 of his caps as a wing-threequarter. He is beautifully balanced runner and a past master of making something out of nothing. He has long been the most dynamic fullback in rugby and takes a lot of pressure off the rest of the French backs because opposing teams need to deploy extra resources to patrol him. Up to the start of this season he has scored a record breaking 29 tries for France including two typically dramatic efforts in the thrilling though unsuccessful French comeback in the First Test against New Zealand this summer. Compared to Gareth Edwards and Gerald Davies who hold the Welsh record of 20 tries – more than anyone from England, Ireland, South Africa or New Zealand has managed, the enormity of Blanco's record can be fully appreciated.

Just as Blanco is the most capped French fullback, so Pierre Berbizier is their most capped scrum-half. By the start of this season he had played 48 times for France and by the end of this season he could have overtaken the world-record total for a scrum-half – the 53 Welsh caps won by Gareth Edwards. He won his first cap for France in 1981 against Scotland when he displaced Jerome Gallion and he has become the successful cog in the very effective French wheel throughout the last nine seasons. He is an outstanding scrum-half in his own right with a fast, crisp, accurate service, a sharp, incisive break and the ability to bury the opposition with a variety of tactical kicks.

Allied to all this he has become the genius in charge of directing and dictating the whole French performance, just as his predecessor Jacques Fouroux did in the late Seventies. France have often had a collection of brilliant individual backs who have lacked a key figure to provide and exploit their collective skills. Fouroux achieved this when he was captain and Berbizier has emulated this in recent seasons. He has been the architect of many dazzling French victories and played a significant role in helping them reach the World Cup final in New Zealand in 1987. He broke his arm in the summer of 1988 in the second international against Argentina and missed most of the first half of last season, but returned to captain France throughout 1989 and remains 'le Patron' in charge this season.

IRELAND

DONAL LENIHAN

BRIAN SMITH

It was thought that the remarkable record of Gareth Edwards of playing 53 internationals in succession would never be beaten, but Donal Lenihan is within striking distance after playing 42 successive matches at lock for Ireland. He won his first cap against Australia in 1981 and he has not only been ever-present in the Irish team in the 1980s, but has toured with the British Lions to New Zealand in 1983, and to Australia in 1989, as well as captaining Ireland in the World Cup of 1987. His wealth of experience at the highest representative level makes it natural for the Irish to build their whole pack around his formidable skills. Last season, with so many relatively inexperienced players, Lenihan did very well in very difficult circumstances to try to rebuild a pack to match the forwards, who helped Ireland to finish at the top of the table in the Championships of 1982, 1983, and 1985, when he was just one of several top-class players. If they are to secure this standard again this season they will need the line-out expertise of Lenihan as one of the best and most aggressive front jumpers in Europe, as well as his strength and skill in the loose. While others find their feet at international level, the single most constant feature in the Irish pack will remain Donal Lenihan. He has an impressive physical presence and he trained fanatically hard to reach peak fitness on the Lions tour to Australia in the summer. He seems determined to be a key forward right through to the 1991 World Cup.

After playing for Australia in the last World Cup, Brian Smith looks destined to represent Ireland in the next. He played four matches for Australia in the 1987 World Cup against America, Japan, Ireland and Wales, and then went on tour to Argentina where he played in the first Test. He is now studying at Oxford University, where he won a Blue in 1988, and is captain of the team this season. He is committed to playing rugby in Britain and Ireland for the foreseeable future and has opted to take his chance with Ireland. Selected for the Irish tour of America and Canada in the summer, he will be a very valuable acquisition for Ireland. One of the most exciting backs in world rugby he played at international level at both scrum-half and fly-half and can also perform at the very highest level at centre and full-back. He benefitted greatly from the outstanding coaching of Alan Jones when he first made the Australian squad, and he quickly developed into one of the most natural footballers in the game. Strongly built, he kicks well with either foot, but has really made his reputation of a well-balanced runner and handler and a shrewd tactician. Clearly forthright in defence and attack, he has precisely the talent the Irish need to bring out the best in the talented backs at their disposal. Just as Lenihan will be their forward linch-pin so Brian Smith will shortly become their key back and quite possibly their future captain.

SCOTLAND

FINLAY CALDER

GARY ARMSTRONG

It seems incredible that two twins should win almost 50 Scottish caps between them and each go on a British Lions tour and yet never play together at international level. Jim Calder played 27 times for Scotland between 1981 and 1985 and toured with the British Lions in 1983. His twin brother Finlay, also a flank-forward, won his first cap in 1986 and had collected a total of 21 caps by the time he was chosen to captain the 1989 Lions tour to Australia. In his first game as captain he guided Scotland to victory over Wales at Murrayfield in 1989 by 23 points to 7 and he was the influential figure both as a player and as captain in helping the Scots to finish joint second in the Five Nations Championship, losing only one match all year and that was to the eventual winners, France. Finlay Calder leads by example from the front and is currently one of rugby's outstanding flankers. He is not only very fast to the breakdown but he has an uncanny instinctive sixth sense with built-in radar which allows him always to be in the right place at the right time. A hard aggressive, physical player in defence, he is at his best in attack. He has great hands which make him highly competitive on the ground, he is a dynamic runner and handler and is a first-class support player. At 6ft 2in he is a useful tail-gunner at the back of the line-out and, along with John Jeffrey and Derek White, makes up a perfect back-row blend which should ensure that Scotland's good run continues.

The product of Jedburgh Grammar School, he rose to prominence very rapidly, playing for Scotland at U–18 and then U–21 level before winning his first cap for Scotland 'B' against Italy in 1987. He celebrated by scoring three tries against Italy and was then selected for a match against France 'B' with Craig Chalmers at fly-half. This partnership was renewed in 1988 when they played for the South of Scotland in the Scottish District Championship. Gary won his first cap against Australia in November 1988 and then played right through the 1989 Five Nations Championship with Chalmers. Like Chalmers, he was selected to tour Australia with the British Lions. He is a protege of former Scotland and Lions scrum-half Roy Laidlaw, who spent a season at the end of his career playing fly-half at Jedforest with Armstrong at scrum-half. Laidlaw has devoted a lot of time helping Armstrong perfect his game and not surprisingly there is a remarkable similarity in style between the two players. Armstrong is a real terrier, always niggling away at his opposite number. He is also very courageous in defence when his forwards provide poor possession. He kicks well from the set-pieces, he is fast and strong on the break and he is a very good support player, whose only weakness at the moment is passing from left to right. Scotland were lucky to have Laidlaw and Rutherford at half-back for so many seasons and they are now equally lucky to have found Armstrong and Chalmers.

WALES

MIKE GRIFFITHS

ROBERT JONES

Amongst the current dearth of top international–class Welsh forwards, it was a great relief to the selectors to have at least one major problem solved by the emergence last season of Mike Griffiths at loose-head prop. From the moment he arrived on the scene he has played a crucial role in bringing considerable stability to a previously rather fragile Welsh scrum. He began life as a very good soccer player with a promising future, but switched codes to play rugby union as a back-row forward in the Welsh team, Ystrad Rhondda. He then joined Bridgend where he quickly proved himself a powerful scrummager, a particularly good support player at the line-out and a surprisingly mobile forward in the open. Last season he made rapid progress when he was selected for Wales 'B' for the match against France 'B' at Brecon in October. The following season he won his first full cap in the game against Western Samoa and became a firm fixture in the Welsh pack for the rest of the season. As a result of several impressive performances for Wales he earned himself a place on the British Lions tour to Australia in the summer. With this added experience he now looks sure to become a bedrock player in the Welsh pack for this season and right through to the 1991 World Cup. He looks set to follow in the footsteps of John Lloyd and Ian Stephens, the two recent Bridgend props who played for Wales with great distinction.

Welsh scrum-halves in the past twenty years have not only lasted a long time at international level but they have also been extremely influential members of the team. It all began with Gareth Edwards (1967–78) and Terry Holmes (1978–85) and it has continued with Robert Jones, who won his first cap at the age of 19 against England and has been a regular first choice ever since. He showed rich promise from a very early age and won twelve caps for Welsh Schools before playing senior rugby for Swansea whilst still at school. He had an outstanding Championship for Wales in 1987 and was a key figure in the World Cup. He struck up a great partnership with fly-half Jonathan Davies in 22 internationals and played a major part in helping Wales to win the Triple Crown in 1988. The following year, at the end of a disastrous season in which the only Welsh championship win was against England in Cardiff, he was selected for the Lions tour to Australia. He was one of the real successes there, quickly establishing himself as the Test scrum-half. He has a very fast, accurate pass off either hand, breaks well and is a strong, well-balanced runner and handler. He is a clever tactician and is also a real tiger in defence. In the Lions' series in Australia he showed great resolution and determination throughout. He looks sure to win many more caps and is capable of emulating the dashing exploits of his famous predecessors, Edwards and Holmes.

Club Preview

BATH RFC : A PROTOTYPE FOR ENGLISH CLUBS
by Nick Cain

Another piece in praise of Bath – yes Sir! – as the man said, "The best is the best, though a hundred judges have declared it so".

In this preview of the domestic club season the spotlight falls on Bath, the 1989 League Champions and Cup winners, the club who landed English rugby's first-ever 'double' – because they provide us with the most complete perspective available on the present and future of the game in this country: the perspective of the pace-setter.

Bath are in the process of playing a key role in the revolution that has been wrought in English rugby since the introduction of a comprehensive competitive league structure just 24 months ago.

In two years the proliferation of clubs has been transformed from an amorphous jelly, which would have had even Quatermass running for cover, into a coherent form which looks suspiciously like the pyramid projected by the Burgess Report all those years ago . . .

No matter, at least we're on our way – Franklin Delano Roosevelt's New Deal had nothing on the way the Courage Leagues have captured the hearts and minds of England's rugby faithful!

The new structure has breathed life into a game that was being starved of oxygen as it fought over its own future, agonising over whether a change in favour of greater competitiveness would ring the first bell in the death-knell of the amateur ethos.

Despite vehement recent proclamations by the RFU that professionalism will be tolerated in no way, shape or form and that "shamateurism" is an unacceptable alternative, there are plenty of indicators winking brightly that tell a different story. The amateur principles of the game are under increasingly heavy fire.

The satisfactory resolution of this issue – i.e. the retention of the amateur ethos in a sport with a growing commercial awareness – remains the key factor confronting the RFU's administrators and the clubs they represent.

To its credit the RFU took a close look at the Bath prototype last season and, while not approving all the plans, particularly the recruitment policy, was mightily impressed with what it saw in organisational terms.

Having asked Bath to make a presentation at a Twickenham seminar for the captains and coaches of the leading Division One and Two clubs, RFU Technical Director Don Rutherford waxed lyrical about the outcome:

"The Bath Plan is simple in outline: they aim to be the best club not only in Britain, but in Europe – their philosophy is if you aim for the stars you may reach the moon.

"They are looking towards Europe (France) for competition because they believe that this exposure will lead to improved standards.

"Bath put a very strong emphasis on good man-management and work hard at creating the sense of a 'family club'. With the senior squad of 1st, 2nd and 3rd XV's augmented by Colts, Youth and Minis sections the playing infrastructure is built on solid foundations."

In more specific terms, the coaching cabal of Jack Rowell, Tom Hudson and David Robson share the work load of administrative/personnel responsibilities relating to the players. This trio have been a cornerstone of the club's success.

Rowell, the managing director of Golden Wonder Foods (Market Harborough), has been the guiding hand behind Bath's domination of the English club scene in the 80s.   Before the introduction of the Courage Leagues, Bath won the John Player Cup four years on the trot ('84, '85, '86, '87), then bowed out of both Cup and League honours in '88 before storming back last season to do an historic 'double'.

Coach Rowell's business management skills have obviously stood him in good stead because he has succeeded with a rota system which has kept up to 18 international players (full and 'B' caps) at the club over this period.

The Bath squad reads like a 'who's who' of the English representative scene and includes the club's first British Lions in Jeremy Guscott, Andy Robinson and Gareth Chilcott. Others in the fold are Stuart Barnes, the current skipper, Simon Halliday, Richard Hill, Graham Dawe, Tony Swift, John Palmer (now retired), John Hall, David Egerton, Paul Simpson and Nigel Redman – all of them England caps – as well as Damian Cronin, the Scotland lock, while stalwarts Richard Lee and John Morrison are both England 'B' regulars. This strength in depth has been reflected in the record books.

Says Jack Rowell: "It's about building up teams, interfacing with people and trying as hard as you can not to let them down. It is the essence of management. Rugby has proved invaluable in trying to help the boys at the club express their potential".

Alongside Rowell, 'the communicator', is Tom Hudson. The sports supremo at Bath University, Hudson is the 'ideas man' in the Recreation Ground set-up. No stranger to controversy, he recently declared his support for the introduction of trust funds for the players.

Working closely with Dave Robson, Hudson has been instrumental in the 'scientific' approach to training at Bath. Some of this has been adopted from rugby league, with Hudson and Robson going 'up north' to glean ideas, with particular emphasis on the use of grid systems to improve passing, tackling and support play. Other influences have come from athletics via the All Blacks.

The fitness level of the Bath squad is regualrly monitored using state-of-the-art methods of assessment – VO2 etc – and a profile of each player is drawn up providing an assessment of their strengths and weaknesses. Coaches and players then discuss the profiles and set targets for the future. While performance on the field is of paramount consideration, the role of the coach extends into such areas as careers advice. This is naturally helped by contacts within the Bath family.

This painstaking forward-planning is also applied to an analysis of fixtures for the new season. Bath draw up their battle plans well in advance, ranking matches in order of importance and arranging training schedules so that players peak accordingly.

Hudson is the architect of such innovative (and costly) moves as the mid-season training camp in Lanzarote. He is also the man behind the recent push for Europe that brought Toulouse to 'the Rec' last season and took Bath to the south-west of France to play Toulouse and Brive as part of their pre-season preparation.

Bath, after the match which clinched their Division One title.

This is a canny move because, as Bath found to their cost in '88, the price of continuous success on the domestic front can be double-edged. In their case fear of losing a proud record gradually led to a more conservative, forward-orientated style, where before they had achieved what Jack Rowell called, 'the rugby version of Ajax's total football'.

Defeat by Moseley in the quarter-finals of the Cup led to a great deal of soul-searching and set in motion last season's emphatic revival and a renewed commitment to "total rugby". With a single blemish on their Division One record – a 15–12 loss to Leicester at Welford Road which they later avenged by beating the Tigers 10–6 in the Cup final at Twickenham - Bath registered six defeats only during the course of the season. Understandably they are looking for new horizons to keep their players on their toes.

At the same time they are providing the rest of English rugby with a model of how the amateur ethos can be balanced against the growing commercial pressures within the game.

The care and attention Bath take with their players has paid off handsomely as they have consistently been able to field sides which play forceful, enterprising, highly successful rugby. Consequently, during the Eighties, they have become one of England's biggest gate-taking clubs (average 6,000) and have encouraged this support by fostering a strong identity with the city and its locality through energetic youth and recruitment policies.

The signing of a three-year £155,000 sponsorship deal with the South Western Electricity Board last February was the product of a great deal of endeavour on and off the field.

There is also the prospect that the club could increase its bank balance by a massive £18 million through the sale of their Lambridge training ground to the Tesco supermarket chain. If the deal comes off it will make Bath into British rugby's first superclub. This rich reward will have been merited in many ways. At their best rugby clubs are self-help societies where the diverse abilities of individuals are given expression and knitted together for the greater good of the team/community.

Bath do justice to that definition and they have built a motor which should fire them towards the millennium as the most successful club in England.

CANDIDATES FOR THE NEW IRISH LEAGUE
by Sean Diffley

The Irish, in the rugby competitive sense, are the last of the Mohicans. True, Tony O'Reilly, in reply to a question at a rugby seminar once, agreed that there was not much competitive rugby in Ireland "... except for the Leinster Cup, the Ulster Cup, the Metropolitan Cup, the Provincial Towns Cup, the Munster Cup, the Connacht Cup, etc, etc, ..."

But, and it has been a very important and contentious ' but', the Irish are the only one of the eight International Board countries without a national competition. There are shoals of provincial competitions, loads of those important schools competitions, but nothing embracing the whole of Ireland.

Prominent playing personalities, notably Fergus Slattery and Mike Gibson, were forever calling on the administrators to do something about the lack of a national competition. They made the case that the national squad needed something more to hone the edges of their game than the surfeit of unimportant friendlies that dominated Irish rugby.

They pointed to the daft situation of international players performing before two men and a dog in a club friendly and on the following Saturday turning out against Wales before 50,000 spectators.

At IRFU level the point has been accepted for several years and the clear success of the leagues in Scotland and England has acted as a fillip to the Irish Union to do something positive. But opposition from many clubs, particularly many of the famous old clubs, has been quite fierce.

Fearing a loss of status that a promotion/relegation league system might bring, they campaigned against the new ideas. It was back in 1985 that the IRFU first proposed an all-Ireland league but the clubs did not back the idea of a two-division league.

Instead there were debates and discussions and counter-proposals and, in the case of many clubs, clear signs of filibustering. In fact, as somebody said, it was all a bit like the medieval schoolmen having one of their ponderous arguments as to how many angels could dance on the head of a pin!

The IRFU was remarkably patient. But just as it was being widely suggested that the Union was prepared to weaken came the news as the 1989 season drew to a close that the IRFU was imposing the national league on the clubs, whether they liked it or not.

So, full marks to the IRFU. A terse announcement said that from "season 1990–91 a national league will be in operation." The clubs to form the National League would be invited to do so and it was made clear that a club, if it felt so inclined, could refuse the invitation.

The clubs selected to form the league would be those whose records in their provincial leagues over the past few seasons entitled them to an invitation.

So, at last the die was cast. Ireland were to join with the other IRFB countries and promote a national competition.

The league will consist of nine clubs in the first division and – for the opening season only – ten in the second division. After that there will be nine in the second division also.

In the first division there will be three clubs invited from each of the provinces of Ulster, Munster and Leinster. In the second division there will be three each from Leinster and Ulster and two each from Munster and Connacht.

A national league may not be the great panacea for all of Ireland's rugby ills but at least its a start.

It is, of course, still far from clear as to which clubs will compose the two divisions. Some famous clubs may not grace the all-Ireland league with their presence at all. Lansdowne, winners of the Leinster league in 1987–88, had a bad run last season and will have to perform very well in the coming season if they are to merit an invitation to the national competition.

One club which almost certainly won't be invited is Bective Rangers who failed to win a Leinster league match last season.

Those who are fancied to qualify for invitations are Ballymena and Bangor in Ulster, Old Wesley and St Mary's College in Leinster, and Constitution and Shannon in Munster. But none can afford to slip up this coming season if they are to make sure.

Last season's outstanding Irish club was Ballymena in Ulster. They won both the Ulster Senior League and the Ulster Senior Cup, doing so with considerable style. Their Cup success was particularly noteworthy. Led by Irish trialist scrum-half, Rab Brady, they beat Collegians by a resounding 46–9 in the semi-final of the Cup and then went on to score a remarkable 25–3 win over the strong Bangor side in the final.

Steve Smith, their Lions hooker, took three strikes against the head in the final and, taking a remarkable season as a whole, they owed a tremendous lot to wing Davy Smyth, who ran in a host of tries, and to fly-half Derek McAleese, whose season's total was 266 points.

At the other end of the country, Ballymena's nearest rivals for the accolade as Ireland's club of the year was the redoubtable Shannon. But the Limerick club, after taking the Munster League title, failed at the last hurdle in the Munster Cup. A victory in that event would have yielded Shannon the distinction of four Cups in a row. But it was not to be. Constitution beat them at Cork, with a penalty goal scored with the last kick of the match.

In Leinster the Lansdowne Leinster Cup triumph owed most to their captain and fly-half, Greg Dilger, with his fine kicking and outstanding tactical sense. Over the full season Dilger scored 277 points. The irony was that Dilger was the only member of the much-honoured Lansdowne back division who was not a representative player.

Answers to 20 QUESTIONS: A RUGBY QUIZ
(see page 92)

RUGBY HISTORY

1   Hartlepool Rovers, 1890.
2   Percy ('Tottie') Carpmael.
3   They are all Founder Members of the Rugby Football Union.
4   Bob Wilkinson. (Barbarians, 1973; Midland Counties, 1983).
5   Brian Price; Gareth Edwards; John Dawes; Mervyn Davies; Phil Bennett; J.P.R.Williams.
6   Oxford University and Glasgow Academicals; captain and full-back was Dan Drysdale (Heriot's FP).
7   Karl Mullen (hooker); 1948.
8   Jacques Fouroux.
9   David Kirk (New Zealand).
10   1960; Cecil Bear.

CLUBS AND PLAYERS

11   Jacques Fouroux; 'Dusty' Hare; D.P.Rogers; Mark Shaw; Ian McLauchlan; Gareth Chilcott.
12   Old Belvedere; Heriot's FP; Kelso; Neath; Newport; Liverpool St Helen's; Metropolitan Police; Gloucester.
13   Gavin and Scott Hastings.
14   Peter Dods and Gavin Hastings each scored 66 points.
15   Chris Laidlaw; David Duckham; Andy Ripley; Phil Bennett;
16   Llanelli; Gloucester; Harlequins; Wasps; Leicester; Hawick; Newport.
17   Both are double internationals (Rodriguez:, Argentina and Australia: Niuqila, Fiji and Australia).
18   Neath and Gloucester (1972).
19   Gareth Edwards; 53 internationals 1966–79.
20   Mike Harrison (England)
     Richard Moriarty (Wales) and Jonathan Davies (Wales against Canada)
     Donal Lenihan (Ireland)
     Colin Deans (Scotland).

AN OPEN FIELD FOR THE SCOTTISH CHAMPIONSHIP
by Bill McLaren

Perhaps the most significant feature of Scotland's sixteenth season of national leagues was the confirmation of a much stronger challenge to Kelso and Hawick, who have dominated Division One for the past six seasons. Kelso did retain the top title but only on points differential, Boroughmuir and Hawick finishing with the same championship points, 20, and there were strong hints that the 1989–90 championship might produce a new addition to the short list of championship winners, Hawick having been champions ten times, Gala thrice, Kelso twice and Heriot's FP once.

Coached by the former British Lions fullback and wing, Bruce Hay, Boroughmuir rued two early reverses at the hands of Selkirk (3–6) and Jedforest (10–22) but in the championship decider on March 25 they beat Kelso at home by 16–10 and clearly now have the stuff of champions. The capital city, indeed, experienced an encouraging revival for there also were signs of revitalisation of Heriot's FP and another famous old former pupils' club, Edinburgh Academicals, who finished fifth and fourth respectively. The Academicals might just have sneaked the title had they been able to beat West of Scotland by 131 points in the play-off of a postponed game! But they lost 14–15. There were glimmerings, too, from two of the less glamorous Border clubs, Jedforest and Selkirk, that they had it in them to stay upsides with the heavy artillery, Jedforest part-inspired by the success as Scotland's scrum-half of Gary Armstrong, Selkirk still seeking due reward from the presence of such distinguished figures as Iwan Tukalo and Iain Paxton.

There were those who reasoned that it was an indictment of the Division One standard that the champions Kelso should have been beaten three times in 13 games. Rather, however, that was an indication of higher overall quality of opposition to them for Kelso remained a very talented side capable of striking on all fronts. Not surprisingly they lost their opening game in the league to Heriot's FP by 13–20 at Goldenacre. Kelso carry a heavy leavening of sons of the soil and harvesting inevitably brings them to the starting gate a touch short of peak fitness. But once they got their wagon rolling they served up some delightful total rugby that had its main launch pad in a superbly blended breakaway trio of John Jeffrey at number 8, Clive Miller and Eric Paxton at flanker, and at their heels two of the longest serving and gifted Border halves in Andrew Ker, capped against Wales and England in 1988, and Bob Hogarth. There was, too, the silken grace at second five-eighth of Roger Baird, scuttling pace from Douglas Robeson, who scored the South of Scotland try against the touring Wallabies in November, and a new challenger to the Scotland fullback berth in the rugged, abrasive, adventurous Marshall Wright, chosen to tour Japan with Scotland in May but missing out through injury. Kelso were worthy champions with 52 tries in 13 games, many of them dazzling scores. Perhaps their biggest disappointment was that, for the second season running as champions, they still lost to Hawick, albeit narrowly by 13–15 and that, having lost the Border League the previous season to Jedforest, they couldn't prevent Hawick from winning it in 1989.

Boroughmuir's record was extraordinary as underlining the considerable influence on their fortunes of one player. Having lost two of their first three league games with a style based in the main on their bulky pack, they recruited a New Zealander, Sean Lineen, who had played for the Counties provincial side there and also had had a season with Pontypool. Lineen so enlivened their training and strategy that in their next four league games they scored 166 points including 28 tries and, in the process, won their away game against mighty Hawick by 26–6. That not only represents the biggest defeat Hawick ever have suffered in 188 national league games but it brought to an end Hawick's remarkable run of 48 consecutive league wins at home. Boroughmuir's disappointment at losing a title they had in their grasp at one stage was eased by the inclusion in Scotland's tour party to Japan of five of their players – Lineen, Brian Edwards (centre), Murry Walker (stand-off and Scotland's top scorer with close on 400 points), and props Grant Wilson and Peter Wright.

For Hawick the season was a huge disappointment with three league defeats and only third place! They still held to a predictable pattern for forward driving and punting halves with not enough faith placed in promising threes of whom Tony Stranger, a powerful wing, toured Japan with the Scottish party, and Nick Bannerman exhibited a feel for space and incision. Hawick again owed much to the prolific boot of Colin Gass, their 35-year-old stand-off, who hoisted his haul in a green jersey to over 2,000 points.

The halcyon time of Edinburgh Academicals, at 132 the oldest club in Division One and unofficial Scottish champions on 23 occasions, were recalled by the admirable upsurge in their fortunes through a highly mobile pack that included Lions' loose-head prop, David Sole, World Cup lock Jeremy Richardson and Hawick's Scotland 'B' captain, Paul Hogarth, alongside the seasoned David Leckie, in the loose-forward unit. Behind them was a revamped youthful back division in which Alex Moore was a powerful wing who had toured with Scotland in Zimbabwe in May 1988, and a talented fullback in Simon Burns who proved a fine points-scorer. Heriot's FP also blended youthful potential in North Midlands scrum-half Mike Allingham, centres David Stoddart and Andrew Stephen and quicksilver fullback Henry Murray, who has played for Scotland 'B', alongside the vast experience of

Peter Hewitt, their top scorer, and internationalist Peter Steven in an exciting back division that at times carried the brand of that renowned exponent of the counter-attack, Andy Irvine, who helped Peter Whitelaw with their coaching.

The campaign also emphasised the coming of age of Jedforest who, with Lions scrum-half, Roy Laidlaw, helping Alan Goodfellow with the coaching, played some of the most fluent rugby of the Championship partly because they had a lightish but mobile pack and partly because they had backs who just loved to run and handle – among them a rich talent at centre in Andrew Douglas who gained district status at just 18, power running from Harry Hogg, injections of pace from Paul Douglas at fullback, who later proved a key figure in Jedforest's sevens successes, at stand-off, and when necessary, a strong, accurate punt from David Shiel, who moved from Melrose to join the Riverside club.

Melrose were the most disappointing. With Scotland's Grand Slam coach, Jim Telfer, as guide, philosopher and slave-driver, and Scotland's new stand-off and veteran centre, Craig Chalmers and Keith Robertson, in a lively back division, they were expected to mount their strongest challenge ever but they flattered one Saturday and deceived the next and it wasn't until March that they gave a clearer indication of their worth with a magnificent 17–3 win that wrecked Hawick's championship chances. Melrose scored three tries to one in that match yet ended their campaign with seven defeats and fifth from bottom in the table. Telfer introduced an additional weekly training session on the Monday night and it was felt that this may have taken the edge off some players. There was no edge missing against Hawick.

The saddest outcome was the demise of a club of massive tradition and accomplishment, Watsonians, who, along with another famous club, Glasgow Academicals, were relegated to Division Two – Watsonians for the first time after 16 years in Division One. Their rivals having gained advantage from 'going open', Watsonians were also hit by the loss to London Scottish of Gavin Hastings, to Waterloo of district number 8 Alan Murray, to Stirling County of astute, long-serving stand-off Gordon Forbes and to retirement of Euan Kennedy who scored one of Scotland's Grand Slam tries against England in 1984. So Scott Hastings had to lead a very young side, lacking physique and know-how, and they were unable to adjust to the pace and power requirements of Division One. They lost all 13 games, leaked a record 520 points and ended with an unprecedented 7–74 defeat at the hands of their arch-rivals Heriot's FP, who ran in 14 tries. Watsonians are a sad loss to Division One, as are Glasgow Academicals, for both clubs are renowned for giving the ball air and can always be guaranteed to enliven the scene. Having decided on a form of limited associate membership, Watsonians surely will not be out of the top division for long.

The success story elsewhere was written by Stirling County who won the Division Two championship with a 100% record over 13 games in which they had a record haul of 391 points. They produced Scotland's top league scorer also in fullback Calum McDonald with 161 points. Stirling County thus completed a promotion sequence unequalled since the days of Highland in Nairn McEwan's time. Stirling's record reads: **1977**: Champions Division 7; **1978**: Runners-up Division 6; **1979**: Champions Division 5; **1980**: Champions Division 4; **1982**: Runners-up Division 3; **1989**: Champions Division 2. Of fondest memory for the County in this latest campaign was their 20–19 defeat of Gala in the match that decided the championship and in which Stirling came from behind twice to beat the Border club for the second year running. With one of the most envied youth organisations at mini and midi level in the Scottish game Stirling County seem to have the back-up to stay in Division One, but in any event they have underlined one of the true values of national league play – its provision of a step-ladder for all clubs that leads from the lower regions to the elite. Not only that but Division One in the coming season will be further enhanced by the return of Gala, champions in 1980, 1981 and 1983, after two seasons in Division Two. They have a sprightly young back division, a dependable marksman and shepherd in British Lion Peter Dods and they will be led by Scotland 'B' scrum-half David Bryson and coached once again by that abrasive character, and fiery flanker of Gala's great days, Johnny Brown.

All of which points to an intriguing search for top honours in the 1989–90 competition that will be launched on September 23 with this fascinating programme: Selkirk v Gala; Stirling County v Stewart's-Melville FP; Hawick v Melrose; Jedforest v Ayr; Heriot's FP v Edinburgh Academicals; Boroughmuir v West of Scotland; Glasgow High Kelvinside v Kelso. And guess who clash in Division Two on opening day? Watsonians and Glasgow Academicals. Some prospect!

John Jeffrey and Eric Paxton offer supprt to Bob Hogarth in a Kelso attack which is threatened by Hawick's Greg Oliver.

A YEAR OF CRISIS FOR WELSH CLUB RUGBY
by Clem Thomas

Once upon a time there was a land populated by ogres and dragons breathing fire, at least that was the way that English rugby players once seemed to perceive Wales. If the visits of the English clubs into the principality were not exactly undertaken in fear and trembling, they were nevertheless journeys which gave cause for anxiety because of the expectation of a good shoeing and little prospect of achieving a victory.

My! How times have changed, English teams no longer fear the dragon's breath and there is no longer any trepidation concerning an excursion over the Severn Bridge. Indeed they often have the temerity to send their 2nd XVs because of their commitment to the Courage League which has rekindled, refreshed and revitalised interest and the levels of play in English rugby.

This new focus, in England, has not only made the old fierce challenge of Welsh rugby redundant but the lack of a competitive structure has made Fleet Street sports editors indifferent to what is happening in Wales. Only if the Welsh Rugby Union's dictum of a league system in September 1990 comes to fruition can the situation begin to change.

The consequences of the lack of leadership by the WRU and the antipathy of the Merit Table clubs to a league system has caused a rift between the two factions, which is still far from resolved. The first meeting between the gate-taking clubs and the competitions committee of the WRU, which took place last May, only hardened the resolve of the big clubs to have nothing to do with the Welsh Rugby Union's plans for a league structure. Apparently so poor was the WRU's presentation that even clubs such as Swansea, Cardiff, Llanelli, who were in favour of leagues and were prepared to break ranks, drew back. Although the Welsh Rugby Union delivered an ultimatum to the first class clubs at the annual meeting in June, the whole matter is still far from clear. The Union holds the whip hand for they could in theory deny dissenting clubs any representation for their players and tickets for international matches.

Consequently the uncertainty and bickering has severely dispirited Welsh rugby in general, which was at a low ebb after the disasters in New Zealand in 1988, and particularly the players who were almost to a man in favour of structured competition.

Welsh club rugby reached a nadir achievement last season, probably the lowest point in its history. They lost more matches to English clubs than one can ever recall, even Llanelli, who together with Neath were the only clubs to deserve the status of being truly first-class, lost three times to Bath who scored more than twenty points against them on each occasion. It was not only poor results that were worrying, it was the general attitudes and style of Welsh rugby which gave enormous cause for concern. Welsh forward play, apart from the rampaging of the Neath pack, was far too static, while the crabbing across field by Welsh backs was appalling. This was even remarked upon by the Lions' party at their get togethers before the Australian tour. Ian McGeechan had to tell the Welshmen to run straight.

Another contemporary view of Welsh rugby comes from Alan Phillips, who at the end of the season retired with honour after 14 years of meritorious service to Cardiff, for whom he scored a remarkable 167 tries, second only to the record of 185 scored by Bleddyn Williams for that great club. Alan was also capped 18 times for Wales and was a British Lion in 1980. He proffers a dire warning to Welsh rugby, maintaining that Welsh fortunes will recede even further unless drastic action is taken. Welsh rugby, he says, must change and the game must be made more attractive to youngsters and there must be a more professional attitude with a small 'p' by the clubs and the Union. In his view players must be allowed sponsorship and fringe benefits outside the game and the clubs must become better organised and more efficient.

It is impossible to ignore the comparison between Wales and England in the last year. The impact made by the Courage League had the energetic and much respected secretary of the Rugby Union, Dudley Wood, describing the 1988–89 campaign as a momentous season.

John Burgess, the past president of the Rugby Union, said at the inception of leagues: "They are not a panacea for the problems of English rugby". He went on to say: "The creation of a democratic playing system enables ambitious and successful players and clubs to progress to the higher echelons of the game and for the less ambitious and talented to find their own level. Furthermore a more competitive playing environment will see players honing their skills and mental approach to the game". These are exactly the attitudes which Welsh rugby needs but of which they are sadly deficient.

It is of huge significance that the improving standards of England and Scotland at international level saw eight English and five Scots players in the Lions team for the last two winning Tests in Australia. Wales supplied only three players, which was their lowest representation in living memory and Ireland none. That neither have a proper competitive structure is surely the final evidence of decline and for the cause of providing league rugby in these two backward countries.

My view is that it is the first-class clubs who are to blame in that they have been more concerned with perpetuating a status which many of them do not deserve and have failed to develop their players and their clubs. Most of them run only one or two sides and do little work outside this narrow confine to develop youngsters. I believe that the Welsh first-class clubs should run at least three sides, a 1st XV, a 2nd XV and a youth team and this should be the bare minimum. If clubs like Berry Hill can field five or six senior teams, four youth sides and a mini-rugby section so can they.

Another Welsh problem is that they have been complacent. Following the glorious Seventies, there has been no leadership from the top and rugby followers in Wales have been grasping at little straws provided by minor, one-off successes such as Wales coming third in the World Cup or the flukey victory over England last season. Welshmen have failed to look at the Eighties as a whole when achievements have been minimal considering that rugby is their national game.

It has been apparent that the WRU has failed to devote sufficient funds to the game because they became obsessed with paying back the loan on their national ground, which was a growing asset but which has proved a bit of a white elephant. They would have been better served by extending the mortgage and spending at least £250,000 per annum on the development of the game over the last ten years, particularly at the junior levels.

There has also been a failure to identify the best players at international level and the time has now come to rethink their selection policies. How for instance could they not have selected Robert Norster for the first two internationals of last season after he had declared himself fit.

Even if Wales do introduce a league system next year they will have an enormous amount of catching up to do. They must however introduce

Colin Laity of Neath is tackled by Llanelli's Nigel Davies

another higher level of competition along the lines of the English Divisional Championship which is nothing less than a series of trials for the England team, or the Scottish inter-district competition which serves a similar purpose.

Apart from the two unrivalled Welsh clubs, Neath, who won the Schweppes Welsh Cup and the unofficial Western Mail Welsh Club Championship, and Llanelli, who won the Merit Table, only Newbridge, Bridgend, Pontypridd, Swansea, Cardiff and Abertillery made any showing last season to win more than 50% of their games.

REVIEW OF THE SEASON
1988–89

THE WHITBREAD RUGBY WORLD ANNUAL AWARDS

Player of the Year	Andy Robinson (Bath)
Senior Team of the Year	Bath RFC
Most Promising Player	Craig Chalmers (Melrose)
Junior Team of the Year	Llanharan RFC
For Services to Rugby	Bill McLaren
The Photograph of the Year	Chris Smith (Sunday Times)
For Services to Journalism	Terry O'Connor (Daily Mail)
Unsung Hero	Paul Rendall (Wasps)
Coach of the Year	Ian McGeechan (Scotland)
Referee of the Year	Clive Norling (Wales)
Umbro Youth Team of the Year	
Schools	Ampleforth School
Colts	Rosslyn Park Colts

1   2   3   4   5   6

MONTHLY AWARDS

November 1988
Senior Team	Nuneaton
Junior Team	Havant
Player	Dewi Morris (Liverpool St Helens)
Welsh Award	Jeff Bird (Maesteg)

December 1988
Senior Team	Rugby
Junior Team	Camborne
Player	Dean Ryan (Saracens)
Welsh Award	Aneterea Aiolupo (Western Samoa)

January 1989
Senior Team	Neath
Junior Team	Scunthorpe
Player	Dean Richards (Leicester)
Welsh Award	Paul Turner (Newbridge)

February 1989
Senior Team	Saracens
Junior Team	High Wycombe
Player	David Pegler (Wasps)
Welsh Award	Mark Jones (Neath)

March 1989
Senior Team	Bath
Junior Team	Bradford and Bingley
Player	Mike Teague (Gloucester)
Welsh Award	Llanelli

April 1989
Senior Team	Llanelli
Junior Team	Old Alleynians
Player	Paul Ackford (Harlequins)
Welsh Award	Bob Norster (Cardiff)

May 1989
Senior Team	Leicester
Junior Team	Rotherham
Player	Dusty Hare (Leicester)
Welsh Award	Neath

1. Craig Chalmers
2. John Willcox, Ampleforth School.
3. Terry O'Connor.
4. Gareth Anderson, Rosslyn Park Colts.
5. Paul Rendall.
6. Ian McGeechan.
7. Howard Perkins, Llanharan RFC, with Cliff Morgan.
8. Chris Smith.
9. Bill McLaren.
10. Clive Norling.
11. Bath RFC.

A SUMMARY OF THE SEASON
by Bill Mitchell

INTERNATIONAL RUGBY

BRITISH ISLES IN AUSTRALIA
JUNE – JULY 1989

TOUR RESULTS

Opponents	Results
Western Australia	W 44–0
Australia 'B'	W 23–18
Queensland	W 19–15
Queensland 'B'	W 30–6
New South Wales	W 23–21
New South Wales 'B'	W 39–19
AUSTRALIA(1st Test)	L 12–30
ACT	W 41–25
AUSTRALIA(2nd Test)	W 19–12
AUSTRALIA (3rd Test)	W 19–18
New South Wales Country	W 72–13
Anzac XV	W 19–15

Played 12 Won 11 Lost 1

TOUR PARTY

Backs
G.Hastings, P.Dods, I.Evans, C.Oti,
A.Clement*, R.Underwood, M.Hall,
J.Guscott, J.Devereux, B.Mullin,
S.Hastings, P.Dean, R.Andrew*,
C.Chalmers, G.Armstrong, R.Jones.

Forwards
D.Sole, B. Moore, S.Smith, D.Young,
G.Chilcott, M.Griffiths, P.Ackford,
W.Dooley, R.Norster, D.Lenihan,
J.Jeffrey, D.White, F.Calder (capt),
D.Richards, M.Teague, A.Robinson.
*Replacement during the tour.

FRANCE IN NEW ZEALAND
JUNE – JULY 1989

TOUR RESULTS

Opponents	Result
Counties	W 24–21
Manawatu	W 28–25
Southland	L 7–12
NEW ZEALAND (1st Test)	L 17–25
Seddon Shield XV	W 39–13
Wellington	L 23–24
Bay of Plenty	W 22–18
NEW ZEALAND (2nd Test)	L 20–34

Played 8 Won 4 Lost 4

ARGENTINA IN NEW ZEALAND
JULY 1989

TOUR RESULTS

Opponents	Result
North Auckland	W 22–16
King Country	W 9–4
Auckland	L 6–61
Wairarapa Bush	W 22–4
NEW ZEALAND(1st Test)	L 9–60
Hanan Shield Districts	W 17–6
Canterbury	L 16–33
Waikato	L 12–30
NEW ZEALAND(2nd Test)	L 12–49

Played 8 Won 4 Lost 4

ITALY IN ARGENTINA
JUNE 1989

TOUR RESULTS

Opponents	Result
Mar del Plata	W 26–9
Cuyo	W 37–22
Rosario	W 27–23
Provincias Argentinas	W 28–24
Cordoba	L 22–30
ARGENTINA	L 16–21

Played 6 Won 4 Lost 2

SCOTLAND IN JAPAN
MAY 1989

TOUR RESULTS

Opponents	Result
Kanto	W 91–8
Kyushu	W 45–0
Japan U–23	W 51–25
Kansai	W 39–12
JAPAN	L 24–28

Played 5 Won 4 Lost 1

ITALY IN IRELAND
DECEMBER 1988–JANUARY 1989

TOUR RESULTS

Opponents	Result
Ireland U–25	L 16–21
IRELAND	L 15–31
Combined Provinces	W 15–14

Played 3 Won 1 Lost 2

ARGENTINA IN FRANCE
OCTOBER–NOVEMBER 1988

TOUR RESULTS

Opponents	Result
Bourgogne	L 15–18
Auvergne	L 19–23
Regional Selection	W 24–15
Regional Selection	W 16–10
Regional Selection	L 22–31
FRANCE	**L 9–29**
Bataillon de Joinville	W 35–15
FRANCE	L 18–28

Played 8 Won 3 Lost 5

AUSTRALIA IN ENGLAND, SCOTLAND AND ITALY
OCTOBER–NOVEMBER 1988

TOUR RESULTS

Opponents	Result
London Division	L 10–21
Northern Division	L 9–15
England 'B'	W 37–9
South–West Division	L 10–26
Midland Division	W 25–18
Combined England Students	W 36–13
ENGLAND	**L 19–28**
Edinburgh	W 25 18
South of Scotland	W 29–4
North & Midlands	W 37–17
SCOTLAND	W 32–13
Combined Services	W 48–7
Barbarians	W 40–22
Italy 'B'	W 26–18
ITALY	**W 55–6**

Played 15 Won 11 Lost 4

WESTERN SAMOA IN WALES AND IRELAND
OCTOBER–NOVEMBER 1988

Opponents	Result	
West Wales U–23	W	19–18
Newbridge	W	16–15
North Wales	W	24–12
Bridgend	L	17–21
Aberavon	L	11–21
IRELAND	L	22–49
Ulster	L	15–47
Connacht	L	18–28
Pontypridd	W	23–22
WALES	L	6–28

Played 10 Won 4 Lost 6

OTHER TOURS

INTERNATIONAL XV IN SOUTH AFRICA
August–September 1989

Natal	W	33–20
President's XV	L	13–36
SOUTH AFRICA	L	19–20
Northern Transvaal	L	19–32
SOUTH AFRICA	L	16–22

WALES 'B' IN CANADA
May–June 1989

Nova Scotia	W	70–3
Ontario	W	23–10
Saskatchewan	W	47–0
CANADA	W	31–29
Alberta	W	53–13
British Columbia	D	21–21

ENGLAND 'B' IN SPAIN
May 1989

Basque XV	W	63–3
Spanish Select XV	W	32–15
SPAIN	W	31–9

UNITED STATES IN ENGLAND
April 1989

South-West Division	L	10–23
Northern Division	L	10–23

NEW ZEALAND MAORIS IN ITALY, FRANCE AND SPAIN
October–November 1988

Littoral Selection	W	22–9
Drome–Ardeche	W	17–12
Pyrenees Selection	D	10–10
Regional Selection	L	25–31
Bataillon de Joinville	W	20–16
French Barbraians	W	31–14

THE FIVE NATIONS CHAMPIONSHIP

Results

IRELAND	21	FRANCE	26
SCOTLAND	23	WALES	7
ENGLAND	12	SCOTLAND	12
WALES	13	IRELAND	19
FRANCE	31	WALES	12
IRELAND	3	ENGLAND	16
ENGLAND	11	FRANCE	0
SCOTLAND	37	IRELAND	21
FRANCE	19	SCOTLAND	3
WALES	12	ENGLAND	9

Final Table

	P	W	L	D	F	A	Pts
France	4	3	1	0	76	47	6
England	4	2	1	1	48	27	5
Scotland	4	2	1	1	75	59	5
Ireland	4	1	3	0	64	92	2
Wales	4	1	3	0	44	82	2

OTHER INTERNATIONALS

WALES	9	ROMANIA	15
ROMANIA	3	ENGLAND	58

The Bledisloe Cup

NEW ZEALAND	24	AUSTRALIA	12

Club, County and Divisional Rugby

ENGLAND

Pilkington Cup
Semi-finals

Gloucester	3	Bath	6
Harlequins	7	Leicester	16

Final

Bath	10	Leicester	6

Courage Leagues Champions
Division One
 BATH   Runners-up: GLOUCESTER
Division Two
 SARACENS Runners-up: BEDFORD
Division Three
PLYMOUTH A Runners-up: RUGBY
Area League North: ROUNDHAY
Area League South: LYDNEY

Toshiba County Championship Final

Cornwall	9	Durham	13

Toshiba Divisional Championship

	P	W	L	F	A	Pts
London	3	2	1	76	33	4
North	3	2	1	45	57	4
South-West	3	1	2	46	43	2
Midlands	3	1	2	34	68	2

University Match

Oxford Univ	27	Cambridge Univ	7

UAU Final

Loughborough	13	Swansea	10

Hospitals Cup

St Mary's	20	London	9

Polytechnics Cup Final

Wales	22	Bristol	3

Inter-Services Champions: The Army
Middlesex Sevens Champions: Harlequins

WALES

Schweppes Welsh Challenge Cup
Semi-finals

Cardiff	12	Neath	19
Llanelli	26	Newbridge	24

Final

Llanelli	13	Neath	14

Whitbread Welsh Merit Table
LLANELLI Runners-up: NEATH

SCOTLAND

McEwans Inter-District Championship

Edinburgh	4	4	0	115	45	8
South of Scotland	4	3	1	93	58	6
Anglo-Scots	4	2	2	89	79	4
Glasgow	4	1	3	56	117	2
North & Midlands	4	0	4	27	81	0

McEwans National League Champions
Division One
KELSO Runners-up: BOROUGHMUIR
Division Two
STIRLING COUNTY Runners-up: GALA

IRELAND

Inter-Provincial Championship

	P	W	L	F	A	Pts
Ulster	3	3	0	46	29	6
Leinster	3	1	2	50	41	2
Munster	3	1	2	46	45	2
Connacht	3	1	2	24	51	2

FRANCE

French Club Championship Final

Toulon	12	Toulouse	18

Fixtures 1989/90

OCTOBER
Wednesday 4th	France v British Isles
Saturday 7th	Toshiba County Championship
Saturday 14th	Cardiff v New Zealand
	Courage Leagues
Wednesday 18th	Pontypool v New Zealand
Saturday 21st	Toshiba County Championship
	Swansea v New Zealand
	Schweppes Welsh Cup 2ndRound
	Leinster v Ulster
	Connacht v Munster
Wednesday 25th	Neath v New Zealand
Saturday 28th	Scotland v Fiji
	Llanelli v New Zealand
	Leinster v Connacht
	Ulster v Munster
	Courage Leagues
Tuesday 31st	Newport v New Zealand

NOVEMBER
Saturday 4th	England v Fiji
	France v Australia
	Wales v New Zealand
	Pilkington Cup 2nd Round
Sunday 5th	London & SE Division v Ulster
Wednesday 8th	Leinster v New Zealand
Saturday 11th	France v Australia
	Munster v New Zealand
	CourageLeagues
Tuesday 14th	Connacht v New Zealand
Saturday 18th	Ireland v New Zealand
	Schweppes Welsh Cup 3rd Round
	Courage Leagues
Tuesday 21st	Ulster v New Zealand
Saturday 25th	Barbarians v New Zealand
	Courage Leagues
	Glasgow v Edinburgh
	South of Scotland v North &
	Midlands

DECEMBER
Saturday 2nd	Midlands v London
	South West v North
	Anglo-Scots v South of Scotland
	Edinburgh v North & Midlands
Saturday 9th	Scotland v Romania
	Scotland'B' v Ireland 'B'
	Midlands v North
Tuesday 12th	Oxford Univ v Cambridge Univ
Saturday 16th	North v London
	South-West v Midlands
	Schweppes Welsh Cup 4th Round
	Anglo-Scots v Edinburgh
	North & Midlands v Glasgow
	Colts County Championship Final

Saturday 23rd	England 'B' v Soviet Union
	North & Midlands v Anglo-Scots
	South of Scotland v Glasgow
Saturday 30th	Glasgow v Anglo-Scots
	Edinburgh v South of Scotland

JANUARY
Saturday 13th	Courage Leagues
Saturday 20th	England v Ireland
	Wales v France
	France 'B' v Scotland 'B'
Saturday 28th	Pilkington Cup 3rd Round
	Schweppes Welsh Cup 5th Round

FEBRUARY
Saturday 3rd	Ireland v Scotland
	France v England
Saturday 10th	Pilkington Cup 4th Round
Saturday 17th	England v Wales
	Scotland v France
Saturday 24th	Pilkington Cup Quarter-finals
	Schweppes Welsh Cup
	Quarter-finals

MARCH
Saturday 3rd	Wales v Scotland
	France v Ireland
	Toshiba County Championship
	Semi-finals
Saturday 10th	Courage Leagues
	Royal Navy v Army
Wednesday 14th	UAU Final
Saturday 17th	Scotland v England
Saturday 24th	Ireland v Wales
	Pilkington Cup Semi-finals
	Royal Navy v Royal Air Force
	Italy Colts v England Colts
Saturday 31st	Courage Leagues
	Army v Royal Air Force

APRIL
Saturday 7th Final	Toshiba County Championship
	Schweppes Welsh Cup Semi-finals
	Wales Colts v England Colts
Saturday 21st	England Colts v France Colts
Saturday 28th	Courage Leagues

MAY
Saturday 5th	Pilkington Cup Final
	Schweppes Welsh Cup Final
Sunday 12th	Middlesex Seven-a-Side Finals